GW01090326

THE PARIS RITZ

Ritz
Ritz
Ritz

THE PARIS RITZ

EDITED BY
MARK BOXER

INTRODUCTION BY
PIERRE SALINGER

THAMES AND HUDSON

Main photography by Patrice Habans, David Massey, Douglas Kirkland and Michael Boys

Editorial Coordinator: Mark Boxer
Designer: William Stoddart
Editor: Stanley Baron
Layout Assistant: Malca Schotten

Typeset in Great Britain by F.M.T. Graphics Ltd.

Printed and bound in Japan by Dai Nippon

CONTENTS

INTRODUCTION by Pierre Salinger

The entrance to the main dining-room of the Ritz, the scene of so many historic, opulent and memorable occasions. In the early 1980s it was completely redecorated and restored in order to revive César Ritz's original conception of a hotel restaurant providing superb food in a luxurious background.

Place Vendôme. Paris. Memories of war and revolution. Memories of victory and defeat. A tall column built out of 1,200 melted cannon seized at the Battle of Austerlitz. And an evolution through centuries from tributes to kings like Louis XV and emperors like Napoleon to a site of unparalleled richness and power. Place Vendôme. The signs of that richness are indelible. There, for all to see, are the fabulous jewelry of Boucheron, of Van Cleef and Arpels, of Bucelatti, or Chaumet. And the signs of power. Place Vendôme. Site of the French Ministry of Justice which rules over France's courts and penal system. The historic and powerful Morgan Bank. Out of the Place Vendôme runs south the Rue de Castiglione towards the plush ancient royal gardens of the Tuileries. North, through the Rue de la Paix, one passes the unique symbol of wealth, Cartier, to one of France's finest symbols of culture, the Palais Garnier, where the greatest voices used to sing the operas of history under a ceiling painted by Marc Chagall. Thus, the Place Vendôme is more than just an ordinary square in an ordinary city. In the museum without walls, which is Paris, it stands out like a bright jewel. And César Ritz with his unlimited dreams chose the right place to install the sumptuous palace that bears his name – the Hotel Ritz. Enter the Ritz. Live its memories, its gilded past. Marcel Proust, the gifted French writer whose novels unveiled in a very special way the life of the rich, adopted the Ritz in his later years as his second home. For an aging man who could no longer travel to the palaces of the Renaissance in Venice and Florence, the Ritz more than filled the void. Remember Coco Chanel, whose haute couture and perfumes dominated the world of fashion. It was living in the Ritz that she collected her inspirations, developed her ideas, received her friends. Now she is dead, but she is remembered. There is a special Coco Chanel suite in today's Ritz. Recall the American writer Ernest Hemingway struggling to achieve fame in the pre-World War II days of his existence in Paris and in Europe. Those were the days when he tried to save up enough money to have one drink a week in the bar of the Ritz now named after him. And after the war, he reached his glory, his fame, and his wealth, and the Ritz became his watering hole. Legend even has it that on the day of the liberation of Paris in 1944, it was Hemingway who liberated the Ritz. Today, a prestigious literary prize bearing his name memorializes his special relationship to the Ritz Hotel. And remember the Kings of England, the Presidents of the United States, the Shahs of Iran, the Maharajas, the Princes, the Begums, that have all flocked to the Ritz during its long and often perturbed lifetime. César Ritz wanted to do more than install a landmark. He wanted to create a hotel that, by its style, its richness, its services, would attract the greats of the world who looked upon Paris as the cultural capital of the world. His success went beyond his dreams. Almost a century after its founding, the Hotel Ritz remains the world's landmark hotel, unique in quality, the first in splendor. And yet the Ritz has lived its years of difficult history. During World War I, a Prussian general who had been refused a table for dinner at the Ritz, tried to level the hotel by lobbing bombs into the Place Vendôme. Fortunately, he failed, only breaking a few windows. During the early years of World War I, the Ritz was partially turned into a hospital. During World War II, the hotel was occupied by the sinister leaders of the Third Reich who, in capturing Paris, profited by taking over its finest hotel. In the mid-1970s, after years of powerful and impeccable leadership by the Ritz family, the jewel which is the hotel began to tarnish. But there is something special about the Hotel Ritz that will not permit it to die. It has too many admirers and devotees, too many people who, in even spending only one night there, have adopted it as their dream palace. And one of them, Mohamed Al Fayed, a powerful Egyptian businessman, bought the Ritz and saved it, bringing it back to its top historic level by investing nearly 100 million dollars. The work of refurbishing the Ritz has been done with a sensitive eye towards the past, with the motive of preserving the special style and service which has marked the hotel since it was founded.

1. THE HOTEL

There is only one internationally famous hotel in all the world whose name, in itself, immediately conjures up an image of exquisite comfort, incomparable service, discreet security and elegant ambience. The Ritz, that jewel in the heart of Paris, is unique in being a symbol as well as a haven for travellers. Even the word "ritzy" has come into the language as a succinct way of describing all that the hotel stood and stands for.

This self-assured distinction is exactly what the founder had in mind in 1896 when he lent his name to the company which was to finance the new hotel. César Ritz reached that point in his life and career after a long training as hotelier, from bottom to top. By the time he opened his luxury hotel in 1898, he was perfectly clear as to how a hotel should be ideally managed, how the rich and illustrious preferred to be looked after, the essentials of a discriminating cuisine; and the years of serious and hard work in his chosen *métier* assured him of a faithful and ample clientele.

The Ritz today, in its modern form, lives up to all its founder's ideals. Any time you enter it is an experience. As César Ritz planned, the first impression is not of a conventional hotel but of a stately yet surprisingly private mansion. He himself liked to call it "a little house to which I am very proud to see my name attached". There is no lobby as such, only a hall of noble proportions with a beautifully carved staircase leading to an upper storey. Copious displays of flowers seem to be everywhere (the monthly budget is 100,000 francs), and contribute to the sense of generous welcome that pervades the reception halls. The Ritz may feel more like a home than a hotel even today because its original building was indeed a private home, belonging to the Duc de Lauzun, who took part in the American War of Independence.

The first person likely to greet the arriving party is the hallman, André Deneux, who began at the Ritz in 1937 as a page. This dapper, bespectacled gentleman started to take all telephone messages in 1942 and has done so ever since. He has a fine memory for the famous people he has seen coming through the revolving doors: Charlie Chaplin, Marlene Dietrich, Humphrey Bogart and Lauren Bacall, Gene Tierney, Barbara Hutton, Randolph Churchill, the Windsors, Richard Nixon, Henry Kissinger.

The Vendôme Bar on the left gives the merest hint of a hotel public room, but here too an atmosphere of private intimacy is created by furniture, carpeting and lighting. As in every part of the hotel, the keynote is discretion.

But the arrivals, if they are not regulars at the Ritz, will be eager to see their rooms or their suites; and it is upstairs that the authentic magic begins. Here is all the excitement of large, high-ceilinged rooms recently decorated to the most exacting standards. Each bedroom, each salon has its own decor, created out of colourful chintzes or heavy silk brocades or satin stripes and gauzes. Each light switch has been designed to order, each door handle and electric fixture shows how much thought has been spent on it. The furniture would be at ease in any home of taste and style.

With all the redecorating that has taken place since 1980, the traditional Ritz touches have been preserved: the marble fireplaces, the gilded mirrors, the Swiss wall-clocks, the monumental carved doors, the walk-in cedar cupboards, and of course the brass bedsteads. Television and radio switches are almost invisibly set into the furniture; and the spacious bathrooms, with marble floors and Ritz dressing gown, fulfil the ideal notions of luxury.

One of the most characteristic aspects of the Ritz is the ease with which its clients' wishes, no matter how personal or complicated, can be satisfied. In addition to the Vendôme Bar, just beyond the entrance, the hotel offers two alternatives on the Cambon side: the Espadon Bar and the Hemingway Bar. On that side also is the restaurant l'Espadon, which has enjoyed a spectacular revival in recent years, both in popularity and in the quality of its food.

Connecting the Cambon and Vendôme branches of the hotel is the long shopping corridor which is probably the most widely known feature of the Ritz. It is generally regarded as César Ritz's last creative contribution before his death in 1918. He suggested that beautiful things should be displayed there, so that a walk along the corridor might be an exercise of pleasure. And so the two walls are lined with vitrines offering for sale an alluring assortment of luxury items from many of the finest shops in Paris.

And aside from these public amenities, any of the twenty-seven room service waiters is prepared to wheel in culinary delicacies on a 24-hour basis. It is easy to feel indulged by all the attention available. This, at any rate, was the intention of the Swiss-born genius who gave his name to this irresistible establishment.

Above, a view of the top floor of the Ritz; in the foreground a portion of the carved column set up in the centre of the Place Vendôme in Napoleon's time.

Opposite, the column seen in all its monumental glory from the balcony of one of the suites recently created on the upper storey of the Ritz, which once consisted of rooms for the clients' personal maids and valets. Crowning the column is a statue of Napoleon in the guise of a Roman emperor.

Place Vendôme, created in the early eighteenth century according to designs by Jules Hardouin-Mansart, was intended as a coordinated architectural setting for an equestrian statue of Louis XIV by Girardon. Mansart, who also designed the Dôme des Invalides and the circular Place des Victoires in Paris, is generally associated today with the "mansard" roof, which was his invention.

The buildings which form the large octagon of Place Vendôme were planned to have an arcaded ground floor with pilasters reaching up to the next two storeys and Mansart's distinctive dormer windows on the top. Each of the four main façades is marked by a pediment, emphasizing the regularity of the overall scheme. Known at various times as Place Louis-le-Grand or Place des Conquêtes, the square ultimately took its

Opposite, two early views of the Place Vendôme, created in the early eighteenth century by the architect Jules Hardouin-Mansart as a spacious frame of buildings for an equestrian statue of Louis IV by Girardon. The statue was knocked down during the Revolution.

pp. 18-31: Details of the interior of today's Ritz Hotel.

name from the Duc de Vendôme (illegitimate son of Henri IV), who lived in a mansion on the site.

The Louis XIV statue, along with other similar commemorations of the Bourbon family, was knocked down during the Revolution, but its white marble pedestal proved useful for displaying the cadaver of a local resident, Le Peletier de Saint-Fargeau, in 1793.

Under the regime of Napoleon, the old monument was replaced between 1806 and 1810 by the present column, which is 44 metres high and based on Trajan's column in Rome. The bas-relief which spirals its surface was created out of cannon captured by the French Revolutionary Army at the battle of Austerlitz (1805). *La Colonne*, as it is known to French history, has been celebrated in song by Dubraux (*"Ah! qu'on est fier d'être français quand on regarde la Colonne!"*) and verse by Victor Hugo (*"O monument vengeur, trophée indélébile"*). This monument, like its predecessor, was also the victim of political conflict. In 1814 the royalists destroyed Napoleon's statue at the top, and in 1871 a group of Commune supporters (including the painter Courbet who was carted off to prison for the offence) pushed over the whole column. After this violent interruption the column was re-erected in 1875 and the statue (of Napoleon dressed as a Roman emperor) set back at the top.

In the course of the nineteenth century, the Place and its appendage, the Rue de la Paix, had gradually become the centre of the luxury trades, and much of that remains today: fashion houses, jewellers, a few banks, shirtmakers, and a hotel, with its discreet awnings bearing the legend "RITZ".

V. ANTIER.
Place Vendôme - Faubg. St. Honoré - 1705.

CÉSAR RITZ
1850 – 1918

VALET

MAID

ESERVE
CHAMPAGNE
RITZ

2. CESAR RITZ, THE FOUNDER

Switzerland has traditionally produced, along with the cuckoo-clocks referred to in the film *The Third Man*, a superior breed of hotel-keepers. It was in that country, in the mountain village of Niederwald, that César Ritz was born in 1850. As in the case of many people of achievement, his was a humble beginning: César was the thirteenth child of Anton Ritz, the mayor of Niederwald, with its mere 200 peasant inhabitants. But the family had lived in the same house since 1778, and boasted among its ancestors a sculptor named Johann Ritz.

A studio photograph of César Ritz, at the height of his success, with an inscription to the great chef Auguste Escoffier, who played a leading role in achieving the immediate success of the hotel when it opened in June 1898.

César may have shown special capabilities even as a child; instead of being prepared for a peasant's life, he was sent to school, and at the age of 15 was apprenticed as a wine-waiter in the Hôtel des Trois Couronnes et Poste in the town of Brig. He was not

successful at this, but was taken on as assistant waiter at a Jesuit seminary in the same town. This too lasted only a short time, and by 1867 he went off to Paris where, since an important Exposition Universelle was taking place, he was likely to find work.

Indeed, he had no difficulty in obtaining a number of jobs, first in a small hotel, then as waiter in a bistro and later in an ordinary *prix fixe* restaurant.

When he was taken on at the fashionable restaurant Voisin, he had reached the first important stage on his way to becoming an accomplished hotelier. Through Bellenger, the proprietor of Voisin, he was introduced to the fine points of providing food to a demanding clientele, and through that clientele he was introduced to the charms and attractions of hobnobbing with the élite. Habitués at Voisin included the likes of George Sand, Sarah Bernhardt, Alexandre Dumas *fils* and the Goncourt brothers. It was people of this sort, as well as those with titles and great fortunes, whom Ritz was to learn to cater for.

During the Franco-Prussian War, he prudently returned to Switzerland, but in 1872 he was back in Paris, working as a floor waiter at the Splendide Hôtel in the Place de l'Opéra, which advertised itself as "one of the most handsomely furnished in Paris". He worked his way in short order to the post of *maître d'hôtel*, but left yet again – this time for Vienna, where another international exposition was taking place. It was as a waiter at the Imperial Pavilion that he is supposed to have experienced his first contact with the Prince of Wales (later Edward VII), who was to become one of his most important patrons.

César's wife later referred to this period as "the years of wandering in the wake of a migratory society".

By the winter of 1873 he was in Nice, as manager of the restaurant of the Grand Hôtel. It was during that first winter on the Riviera that he met the director of the Rigi-Kulm Hotel in Switzerland, a Herr Weber, who invited him to work there the next

The first enlargement of the Ritz took place before the First World War when a property at 38 Rue Cambon was bought and joined to the Place Vendôme nucleus. The two photographs at left show this work in progress during the early Spring months of 1911.

César Ritz with his two sons, René and Charles. René, the favourite, died tragically in 1918, shortly before his father. Charles, a wanderer at heart, eventually assumed his father's mantle and steered the hotel through difficult times in the 1950s and '60s.

summer. He proved to be a popular and resourceful manager of the Rigi-Kulm restaurant, and came to the attention of one of the guests, Colonel Maximilian Pfyffer d'Altishofen, who was to play an interesting role in his career. Pfyffer was an architectural engineer who had recently designed the Grand National Hotel, owned by his father-in-law, on Lake Lucerne. Impressed by what he saw and heard of César Ritz's abilities, Pfyffer made a note of the name for future reference.

In the meanwhile Ritz served a period at the Grand Hotel Locarno, and the next winter and the winter after that he was in San Remo. At the Hôtel de Nice he had his first taste of handling financial administration; he managed to double the hotel's turnover in a single season. At the Hôtel Victoria, frequented by tuberculosis patients, he became acutely interested in the problems of hygiene and sanitation. His observations led him to disapprove of heavy furnishing materials that could be cleaned only at rare intervals; all fabrics must be washable, and he decided that paint was preferable to wallpaper. He was determined that if he were ever to have a hotel of his own, every bedroom would have a private bathroom. This was an idea well in advance of his time.

While he was running the Victoria, Ritz received a visit from his old client Col. Pfyffer, who told him that the Grand National at Lucerne was in difficulties. Pfyffer asked Ritz to take over management of this important luxury hotel, and Ritz accepted the offer. Under the young man's guidance (Ritz was only 27 when he took on the job) the Grand National became one of the most elegant hotels on the continent. His wife recorded later that "great ladies such as the Duchesse de Rochefoucauld, the Duchess de Maille, the Comtesse Greffulhe, Lady Leache, Lady Greville, the Duchess of Leeds and the Duchess of Devonshire, actually appeared in the public ballrooms and dining room and lent their enthusiastic support to the special fêtes which Ritz organized." In the course of eleven summer seasons at Lucerne, Ritz was gradually making a name for himself, particularly with the arbiters of society who were to become his leading customers.

During the winters, he managed various hotels in the South of France. In Mentone, he met the young girl Marie-Louise Beck, whom he married in 1887 and who was to have a strong hand in the success of the Ritz Hotel. But the endlessly active César still had many rungs to climb on his ladder to that ultimate success. For a time he owned and ran the buffet of the Jardin d'Acclimatation in the Bois de Boulogne. An old friend

Édification d'un Hôtel à Voyageurs
15. Place Vendôme 15. à Paris.

Composé d'un bâtiment en aile, élevé sur cave ou sous sol (et partiellement au 2ème Étage de cave), d'un rez de chaussée, de quatre étages carrés et de deux étages dans le comble. —

Entre les soussignés: Monsieur César Ritz, Directeur de The Ritz Hotel Syndicate Limited, dont le siège est à Londres et agissant au nom de la dite Compagnie, demeurant à Londres à Savoy Hotel, mais faisant élection de domicile en l'immeuble de la Société, 15. Place Vendôme à Paris d'une part, et Monsieur A. Ruelle, fabricant de stores, demeurant à Paris, 53. Rue des Petits Champs, d'autre part; il a été convenu et arrêté ce qui suit: The Ritz Hotel Syndicate Limited, propriétaire d'un terrain sis à Paris, 15. Place Vendôme et voulant y faire élever une construction à usage d'hôtel, a fait dresser par Monsieur Mewès, architecte à Paris 36. Boulᵈ des Invalides, les plans, élévations et coupes, cahier des charges et devis descriptifs, clauses et conditions à remplir pour l'exécution des travaux. Ces pièces approuvées par le Directeur de The Ritz Hotel Syndicate Limited ont été communiquées à Monsieur Ruelle qui en a pris connaissance et qui déclare avoir fait tous les mesurages, calculs et vérifications nécessaires pour se rendre compte de l'importance des travaux et de leur valeur, qu'il aurait à exécuter pour arriver à l'entier et complet achèvement de la construction en ce qui le concerne. —

Monsieur Ruelle s'engage tant en son nom qu'en celui de ses représentants, successeurs et héritiers, envers The Ritz Hotel Syndicate Limited, représenté par le Directeur soussigné qui l'accepte, à exécuter les Stores, suivant toutes les règles de l'art et avec la dernière perfection en se conformant aux pièces signées par l'Architecte et le représentant de The Ritz Hotel Syndicate Limited qui lui seront remis en signant le présent marché. L'Architecte ou son inspecteur sur le chantier aura le droit de refuser tous les matériaux qui seraient défectueux, ou n'auraient pas les qualités ou dimensions prescrites ou acceptées et aussi de faire démolir et remplacer tout ouvrage jugé mal exécuté et non recevable, et ce, sans aucune indemnité au profit de l'entrepreneur; la surveillance s'étendra jusqu'à la police du chantier et donnera le droit à l'Architecte ou à son inspecteur de demander à l'entrepreneur tout changement dans son personnel.

from his early days at the Splendide in Paris offered him a tempting partnership in a hotel at Trouville. Although Ritz succeeded in making the hotel popular with gourmets, the shortness of the holiday season resulted in severe financial problems. He had to become an employee again, this time as manager of the Grand Hôtel in Monte Carlo. He took with him the chef from Trouville, only to have him lured away by the Hôtel de Paris.

At that point he sent for Auguste Escoffier, and the substitute turned out to be a greater chef than the original. Thus began a mutually profitable relationship which lasted to the turn of the century. César had first heard of Escoffier in about 1870, when General MacMahon discovered him as chef of the Petit Moulin Rouge in Paris and sang his praises. Now, some fifteen years later, Ritz and Escoffier began to develop together a blueprint for what an exclusive luxury hotel should be, with the emphasis on comfort, cuisine and service.

When Queen Victoria was vacationing at Mentone, she and her Scottish gillie, John Brown, dined several times at the Grand in nearby Monte Carlo. In the early 1880s the Prince of Wales reserved a suite of rooms there and on his arrival asked Ritz to arrange the menu: "Something light, but interesting!" The reputation of Escoffier's talents spread far enough to attract the *beau monde*; one frequent visitor was the Gilbert and Sullivan impresario, Richard D'Oyly Carte, who was planning to build a hotel in London and had hopes of persuading Ritz to share his dream.

In 1887 Ritz relinquished his activities in Monte Carlo and Lucerne, and acquired the Hôtel de Provence in Cannes. He also took on management of the Restaurant de la Conversation, as well as a small hotel in Baden-Baden, the Minerva. The German Emperor attended the opening night of the restaurant in Baden-Baden, and the Prince and Princess of Wales, with their five children, stayed at the Cannes hotel for several weeks in 1888.

Agreement between the Ritz Hotel Syndicate Ltd (London) and the builder A. Ruelle (53 Rue des Petits Champs, Paris) for the construction of a four-storey hotel at 15 Place Vendôme in accordance with plans executed by M. Charles Mewès.

And now D'Oyly Carte's new hotel, the Savoy, was nearing completion in the heart of the London theatre district where he had made his fortune. Built between 1884 and 1889, the Savoy incorporated the most up-to-date American techniques, including fireproof construction with steel joists encased in concrete, electric lights (at "no charge"), lifts (called "Ascending Rooms") and numerous bathrooms. Hotel architecture was advanced in the United States because of the great mobility of American society, the longer distances between urban centres, and the relative scarcity of the type of family hotel to be found in Europe.

Having seen the accomplished way Ritz entertained his resplendent clients, D'Oyly Carte was determined to talk him into forming some association with the new Savoy. According to Ritz, D'Oyly Carte approached him at Cannes in 1888: "He wants the *clientèle* I can give him, the people who come here, who go to Baden, who were my patrons at Lucerne and Monte Carlo: the Marlborough House set – Lord Rosebery, Lord and Lady Elcho, Lord and Lady Gosford, Lord and Lady de Grey, and the Sassoons, the Roman princes, Rudini, the Crispis, the Rospigliosis, the Radziwills, and so forth; the best of the theatre and opera crowd – Patti, the De Reszkes, Coquelin, Bernhardt; the Grand Dukes and the smart Parisian crowd – the Castellanes, the Breteuils, the Sagans; he wants the Vanderbilts and Morgans, he wants the Rothschilds. He wants to make his hotel the *hôtel de luxe* of London and of the World."

D'Oyly Carte's dream was fully realized. The wealth that was pouring into London from Asia, Africa and America created a new way of living that was lent style and distinction by the presence of the royalty and aristocracy of Europe. The spectacular success of the Savoy owed everything to the genius of César Ritz and to Escoffier, who offered the British the exquisite delights of French *haute cuisine.*

Between them, Ritz and Escoffier, when they came to run the Savoy in 1889, introduced into England the novel concept of the hotel restaurant as an acceptable social venue. At that time people of quality or respectable standing were not likely to dine with any regularity in public restaurants. Entertaining, in an era of cheap and copious service, was undertaken mainly at home. But Ritz managed, with the help of his long-time patron, Lady de Grey, and later through the frequent visits of the Prince of Wales, to create an unmistakable vogue for dining at the Savoy. His well-placed clients also helped to alter the restrictive licensing laws so that the restaurant could serve meals and wine on Sundays and remain open beyond 11 p.m. on other nights.

Lady de Grey, a leader of London society and a notable beauty, was one of the influential clients and supporters of César Ritz in his early days.

Ritz's career at the Savoy lasted nine years, but during that period he was involved in a number of other hotel enterprises in a wide compass that included Rome, Frankfurt, Monte Carlo, Salsomaggiore, Wiesbaden, Biarritz, Lucerne, Mentone and even Palermo. His wife, who with their first-born son Charles often shared his journeys, wrote of that peripatetic epoch that "César's suitcases were never completely unpacked; he was always just arriving from or departing on a new journey." Although this excess of work and travel began to have a bad effect on his health, he was driven by his obsessive ambition to create a superb hotel of his own in Paris.

Even before he left the Savoy, in circumstances which are not clear, plans to achieve his ambition were already afoot. Ritz's certainty that there was a need for the "perfect" hotel that he envisaged in Paris was fortified by the rich clients who had been flocking to the Savoy, many of whom had made their fortunes through diamond- and gold-mining in South Africa. These people being prepared to lend their financial support to

Ritz's venture, a company was formed on 28 May 1896, called "The Ritz Hotel Syndicate Limited", and registered under the signatures of César Ritz, five members of his personal team at the Savoy (Escoffier, the *maître d'hôtel* Echenard, the cashier Agostini, the staff manager Baumgartner, César's private secretary Collins) and the outsider H.V. ("Harry") Higgins, a barrister of means who had been a long-time supporter of César's. The original documents show that Ritz had already hit upon "a piece of land in the Place Vendôme, in the City of Paris"; it was, in fact, No. 15, most recently occupied by the bank Crédit-Mobilier. And Ritz, even before making sure of his prospective backers, had bought an option on the property with money borrowed from Marnier Lapostolle, the manufacturer of the liqueur that came to be known as Grand Marnier.

César's backers, who included the Armenian oil magnate Calouste Gulbenkian and the South African multi-millionaire Alfred Beit, raised various objections about the size of the site and its location, but Ritz was a past master in the arts of persuasion. On 15 October 1896, a summary of the capital and shares of the Ritz Hotel Syndicate recorded that the nominal capital of £120,500 was divided into 24,000 ordinary shares with 100 deferred. Of the total, 16,346 ordinary shares had been taken up and the principal shareholders included Sigismund and Ludwig Neumann (2,000 and 1,000 respectively); Baron Jacques de Gunzbourg (1,600), Robert Crawshay (1,000) and the banker Leopold Hirsch (500). César Ritz was credited with 6,000 ordinary and 80 deferred shares, and Escoffier with 400 ordinary. The remaining deferred shares were held by Ritz's fellow directors – Earl de Grey, the Prince of Wales's shooting friend; Harry Higgins; and Arthur Brand, a partner in Lazard's Bank. It was all very British, and even the minutes of the board's meetings were taken in English until the mid-1920s when they suddenly switched to French. The Marquis d'Hautpoul, who lived in England and was married to a Stonor, joined the board in 1899.

Marie-Louise Ritz, the girl César first met in Mentone and married in 1887, proved to be the perfect helpmate. Not only did she travel far and wide with him during the period before the Ritz was founded, when he had multiple interests in many parts of the Continent, but she took over the reins of management when he began to fail in 1902 and carried on until 1953.

AUGUSTE ESCOFFIER, a dapper man of diminutive stature, was the dominant chef of his day. His original and creative approach to the artistry of cooking and the production of exquisite meals in quantity still leads experts to rank him as one of the greatest figures in his profession.

Mme. Ritz, in a memoir she wrote after her husband's death, paid handsome tribute to the man who shared in making such a success of the Ritz Hotel: "During the first years Ritz spent at the Grand Hotel National in Lucerne he had evolved almost completely his ideas of what a *de luxe* hotel could and should be, and had been convinced of the importance in such a hotel organization of superb *cuisine.* Until he met Escoffier he had not yet been able perfectly to apply his ideas in that realm. And as to Escoffier, until he met Ritz no one had fully appreciated his talents or given him full scope to exercise them."

Auguste Escoffier, the culinary genius of turn-of-the-century Paris, established the restaurant of the Ritz. His association with César began at the Grand Hôtel in Monte Carlo. They later operated together most successfully at the Savoy Hotel in London between 1889 and 1896.

Although Escoffier was a brilliantly inventive chef, he was unconventional in concerning himself with the digestive properties, as well as the chemical content, of food. No one before him had explored means of preserving cooked food, and especially of preparing certain sauces in large quantities.

He took as much delight as any major chef in devising elaborate settings for his dishes, but the actual preparation of food was much simpler in his kitchens than was usual in the Belle Epoque.

One of his most practical contributions was to clean up the traditional inferno that passed for a restaurant or hotel kitchen in his day, and to introduce the rationalization of kitchen tasks into specific sectors. This made for increased efficiency, and his suppression of brutality against apprentices led to improved morale.

When it came to the freshness and quality of the ingredients that went into his dishes, Escoffier was uncompromising. He had a passionate predilection for the products of Normandy: its eggs, butter and cheese, vegetables, and fish, all seemed – then as now – particularly delicate and flavourful. He insisted that only Norman butter be used in cooking.

Escoffier's brilliant career encompassed an era during which an important social change was taking place. People in society were beginning occasionally to entertain groups of friends and acquaintances in public restaurants rather than at home. One contributing cause appears to have been womens' demands to enjoy the same amenities that their husbands did. This delighted Escoffier, who adored women, understood them and enjoyed catering to their tastes. He acknowledged that many of his best dishes were created for women, and he was prone to name them for the great divas, actresses and beauties of the day: salade Réjane, mignonettes de caille Rachel, poire Mary Garden, coupe Yvette, poularde Adelina Patti, fraises Sarah Bernhardt, peches, poires and coupe Melba.

Today no serious student of *cuisine* is unaware of Escoffier's *Guide Culinaire.* It is more than an essential and enlightening cook book; it is a reflection of his times, and a guide to his passage through many of the great kitchens in Europe.

Olivier Dabescat, the legendary *maître d'hôtel* of the Restaurant for something like sixty years, was responsible for setting the high standards of service provided by the hotel, just as Escoffier set the standards in catering. Olivier was a Basque who began his hotel career, when he was only twelve years old, in London. By the time he came to the attention of César Ritz, he was managing the Paillard Restaurant in Paris, and a year after the Ritz opened, he was invited to take charge of its restaurant.

Suave and monocled, he became famous for the finesse with which he exercised his considerable power. Although he was an inveterate snob in his attitudes towards people with titles and social standing, he was also invaluable to the hotel by developing an instinct for recognizing and showing flattering deference to those clients with the thickest wallets. And yet he would not, for example, tolerate the drunken antics of James Gordon Bennett, millionaire owner of the *New York Herald* and its Paris offshoot. Bennett had been forced to leave New York because of a particularly disgraceful case of public misbehaviour, and he proved to be no less violent and obnoxious once he settled in Paris. When he started to smash glasses in the Ritz Restaurant, Olivier was at no loss: he simply bundled Bennett off to Maxim's, or some similar establishment, with the assurance that the atmosphere was much livelier there.

He was described by George Painter as being

Tall, handsome, distinguished, and slightly sinister; in his devoted genius for his profession he displayed the sanctity of a high priest, the tact of a diplomat, the strategy of a general, and the sagacity of a great detective. "I have given Monsieur the best table," he would whisper, a dozen times each evening, whenever a favourite client entered.

Olivier was immensely proud of his royal clients, among them the Prince of Wales, Alfonso of Spain, the Shah of Persia, Manoel of Portugal, and the various Russian Grand Dukes. But he was sufficiently devoted to the hotel's interests to make sure that a choice table was always available for the vulgar but rich widow of John Mackay, the King of the Comstock. He was not perturbed by eccentric clients with their pets. Berry Wall, for instance, invariably dined with his chow dog suitably dressed in a dinner jacket. The chow's stiff collars and black satin stocks were made by Charvet from the same pattern as Wall's. Olivier attended to the dog's preferences, just as he produced live rabbits for the Marchesa Casati's boa constrictor and live pigeons for Mrs McLean's hooded falcon. On Christmas Day 1900 another eccentric American visitor challenged Olivier's claim that he could supply anything his clients might order by asking for elephant's feet. Olivier duly bought an elephant from the Paris Jardin des Plantes and served up the four feet to the American's party. He also kept back a small portion for Calouste Gulbenkian's table where the oil magnate's four-year-old son Nubar had been watching, all agog. It tasted, Nubar said, "like something between sponge and flannelette."

The formidable Olivier towards the end of his long career at the Ritz.

The Gulbenkians maintained a large suite at the Ritz overlooking Place Vendôme, Calouste being a specially honoured guest because of his early financial support for César Ritz. This mysterious and reclusive man had virtually no friends. Olivier was one of the few people who knew him well. He only once made the mistake of asking the millionaire for advice about investments, for he learned that in such circumstances Gulbenkian always advised the opposite of what he did himself.

Olivier was so ubiquitous that he inevitably turned up in various memoirs, and he was presumably Proust's model for the headwaiter at "Balbec".

3. "THE LAST WORD IN ELEGANCE"

Ritz's brilliant notion in buying 15 Place Vendôme was to construct his hotel behind the existing late-17th-century Mansart façade within a private mansion. While he was determined to take advantage of the latest technical improvements, he particularly wanted to avoid anything like the purpose-built "Grand Hotels" of his time. It would be, he said, "the last word in elegance", as well as in modern hygiene, efficiency and beauty.

The famous Ritz restaurant, after the First World War, with a view towards the garden that runs alongside the hotel. The management have always placed great emphasis on the use of plants and flowers for elegant decoration.

The architect he chose to realize his vision, Charles Mewès, talked him out of the idea of being superficially "modern" and drew up a plan for a series of spacious and attractive rooms, all with appropriate furniture, carpets, hangings and chandeliers in the various classical styles of French interior design from late Louis XIV to the First Empire.

Mewès, described as recently as 1947 in a British architectural journal as "the best type of the intellectual and well-bred Frenchman", was a successful product of the all-powerful Ecole des Beaux-Arts. By the time of his collaboration with Ritz he had already completed a number of highly regarded commissions and was at the summit of his career. Their partnership in constructing the hotel was remarkably fortunate. César admitted to his wife that he had no knowledge of architecture and little of decoration: "I know what I need for perfect efficiency and elegance in the hotel I want but I haven't the least idea how to create it." But the two men recognized the perfectionist in each other, and when Mewès said to Ritz that the hotel's beauty must be of the sort that would last for ever, their agreement was complete.

No detail was too small for their attention. For example, César had every other armchair in the dining-room equipped with a small brass hook on which ladies could hang their purses. All the counterpanes used on the beds had to be lightweight and quilted so that they could be washed easily, and every mattress had a chamois slip-cover. Three main colour schemes were worked out; blue, white and grey for rooms facing south; champagne yellow for the rooms facing north; and various shades of pink wherever daylight happened to be scarce. Upholstery was equally light in spirit; in ladies' bedrooms Watteau pinks and blues predominated, while so-called bachelors' rooms were outfitted in various shades of plum. The furnishings were reproductions of Louis XV and Louis XVI pieces, painted to complement the walls. Instead of the flamboyant wallpaper and the rich brocades which were all the rage in the Belle Epoque, the bathrooms and bedrooms in the Ritz were covered with flat Dutch paint in the best 18th-century tradition.

Ritz chose fitted cupboards rather than the conventional wardrobes which were dust collectors. He installed brass bedsteads on the grounds that they were hygienic. Hours were spent testing and adjusting electric fittings and bulbs; César insisted upon pleated lampshades and had them lined with a layer of pink silk in order to cast a more flattering glow. He was particularly interested in the novelty of concealed electric lighting and pioneered a special restaurant table-lamp that lit the food without blinding the customer. This was all at a time when, as Mme Ritz observed, "the last word in artistic lighting was considered to be a bronze nymph holding up a cluster of naked light-bulbs in place of flowers". Another of Ritz's notable achievements was those lights that click on and off automatically in walk-in cupboards.

In preserving the external appearance of the building, Mewès permitted himself one licence when he opened up four of the six arches so as to provide access for carriages up to the front doorway. The high, austere, stuccoed hall within conformed to Ritz's wishes not to have a large lobby, as was common in most contemporary hotels. Ritz considered that a spacious area near the entrance encouraged undesirable "loiterers".

The outer hall gave on to a writing-room, decorated and furnished in the Louis XVI style, which overlooked an attractive Winter Garden with a Trianon-style fountain and a rotunda in Languedoc rosy pink. The long corridor, with the gardens on the left, ran along through the oak-panelled inner hall, where tea was served, to the "sanctuary" of the hotel, the dining-room. Large windows overlooked the gardens and the beauty of the room was enhanced by the reflection of the enormous mirrors. The carpet, manufactured by the Maison Braquerie, was based on an old drawing supplied by Mewès.

A correspondent for the London magazine *Truth* described the bedrooms:

Overleaf: Two of the decorated menus (1900 and 1909) which were produced for special occasions at the Ritz Restaurant.

Were I afraid of catching tuberculosis – the most contagious of diseases – I should go the Hotel Ritz. Every bedroom faces south and has wide windows that solicit light. There are no bed curtains. The window curtains are of white muslin, so as to be often washed. The white walls would show the least

THE NORTH POLE

MENU

Hors-d'Œuvre à la Russe
Caviar frais d'Astrakan
Melon frappé
Tortue claire
Consommé Pôle Nord
Filets de Soles au Champagne
Laitances Pimentées
Selles d'Agneau de lait à la Grecque
Aubergines
Canard de Rouen Vendôme
Sorbets au Monopole
Terrine Sainte-Alliance
Salade Washington
Fonds d'Artichauts au Velouté
Soufflé au Parmesan
Poires Cressanes, Friandises
Corbeilles de Fruits

Vins

Cocktails - Xérès
Château Caillou 1888
Château Laffite 1875
Heidsieck Dry Monopole 1892
Château Yquem
Grande Fine Champagne "Ritz" 1790

HOTEL RITZ

JULY 9TH 1900

1er Janvier 1909
Menu
Caviar et Blinis
Crème de Maïs
Tortue claire
Filets de Sole à l'Américaine
Selle d'Agneau de Pauillac à la Broche
Haricots verts nouveaux
Pommes fondantes
Bécasses au Fumet
Salade Diplomate
Asperges vertes sauce Mousseline
Ananas voilé à l'Orientale
Friandises
Corbeilles de Fruits.
– Palermo –
Enero 1º 1909
Vauclin Paris
Ritz Paris

speck of dust, so would the highly-polished furniture. I cannot think where a microbe could take refuge, unless in the carpets; and even there the oxygen from the great continuity of gardens and the southern sunlight must soon make short work of them.

The bedcovers were satin in plain colours of old rose, green, salmon, mauve or blue. The fitted carpets in the bedrooms tended to be in light colours with a single-tone design overseen by Mewès and executed to order. Lamps were in the shape of a crystal bowl. The chimneypieces were generally furnished with two china vases. The inevitable Swiss clock, decorated in bronze and pearls, hung on the wall. These timepieces, which work by compressed air, have always been a special feature of the Ritz, along with the violin-handle light switches.

The official opening took place on 1 June 1898, in spite of a number of last-minute crises. Two weeks before, the tables and chairs of the dining-room, the *pièce de résistance* of the hotel, had not been delivered. Then, when the careful cabinetmaker had been persuaded to release his handiwork a week later, Hans Pfyffer, a son of Ritz's early benefactor, put another idea into César's head. Pfyffer tested one of the rose brocade-covered chairs and found it comfortable as well as beautiful, but he thought it a pity that at least half of them had not been made as armchairs. Thus seven days before the opening, Mewès had to design suitable arms to be fixed to several dozen chairs.

And on the very morning of the opening, both Ritz and Mewès decided that the dining-room tables were too high. They were sent back to the manufacturer straight away so that a couple of centimetres could be cut off their feet.

But by the evening everything was ready and the Place Vendôme was filled with equipages finding their way to the entrance of No. 15. Behind a row of powdered footmen in the arcade stood the diminutive, impeccably dressed figure of César Ritz.

Overleaf: A view of Place Vendôme at the turn of the century.

And a gratifying number of the clients he had grown to know and cultivated during the years of preparation came to do him honour. Mme Ritz enumerated them later when she wrote of the glittering event: "Exquisite Boni de Castellane . . . Comtesse de Pourtalès, looking like a stately swan in a gown of trailing white . . . Grand Duke Michael with Countess Torby, for whose sake he lived in exile from the Russian Court. Mrs William Corey . . . among our first distinguished American patrons . . . The Rothschilds were there *en masse*."

When the guests left this unique "first night" it was nearly dawn. Mme Ritz and her contented husband walked out into the Place Vendôme: "standing by Napoleon's great column, we looked at the hotel my husband had created and talked about its future until the sun came up. Just before we started back he said, 'Mimi, we have two sons. This hotel will be our daughter; and if anything should ever happen to me, please take good care of her.' "

Charles, the elder of the Ritz boys, was not on the best of terms with his mother and decided as a young man that he had no taste for the hotel business. All his life he felt a special attraction for the United States and in 1916 his mother bought him a passage to New York and gave him $100. He roamed the country, finding work in American hotels. Then in 1918 he enlisted in the American Army, and became a sergeant. He later toured the country selling music boxes, and even tried producing motion pictures in New Jersey, which was not a very successful venture. Although the adult Charles Ritz's principal loves remained fly-fishing and toy trains, he finally accepted the destiny thrust upon him by his descent.

In 1927 he returned to the Ritz; and eventually he exhibited considerable panache and inventiveness in maintaining the legacy he had not been able to escape. Charles Ritz's younger brother, René, a gifted and promising son by all accounts, died tragically of spinal meningitis in 1918.

Overleaf,
The Ritz Restaurant a few years after the hotel was launched.

If César Ritz looked on his hotels as children, there were further offspring after the triumph in the Place Vendôme. His next major involvement was in the Carlton Hotel in the Haymarket in London. He left the Ritz in the capable hands of his well-trained management staff – Henry Elles (who had been restaurant manager in the Savoy days), Victor Rey, and Olivier Dabescat as *maître d'hôtel* – and proceeded to transplant onto the Carlton all that he had learned in preparing the Ritz.

He called on Charles Mewès to design the principal interiors. At great expense the floor of the Palm Court was made lower than that of the dining-room, with a fine open staircase connecting the two, "so that the ladies entering the dining-room or leaving it may do so dramatically," as Ritz explained. According to Mme Ritz, he deliberately created the interiors with the Prince of Wales's tastes in mind. These attentions were not unrewarded and the Prince dined publicly more than once in the restaurant, which offered Escoffier's enterprising *à la carte* menus at the now fashionably late after-theatre hours. Upstairs there was a bathroom attached to every bedroom for the first time in any London hotel.

It was in the lovely Louis XVI setting of the Carlton, with its palms and mirrors, that César Ritz, in the midst of elaborate preparations for what was to have been the most spectacular London season of all time, heard the shattering news on 24 June 1902 of the postponement of Edward VII's Coronation. Pale and stricken, Ritz announced the information to the diners in his restaurant. His Majesty was at that moment undergoing an emergency operation for peritonitis.

Ritz had been overworking as usual on the proposed festivities for 26 June; not long before, he had returned early to his home at Golders Green, in the northern suburbs of London, complaining of fatigue. "We might as well face it," he told his wife, "I am an old man now."

He was in fact not yet 52.

The shock of the Coronation postponement, which touched on so many plans he had made at the hotel, precipitated a nervous breakdown from which Ritz never fully recovered. In 1903 he had a second breakdown. According to his wife, he "gradually sank out of life. A dark cloud seemed to envelop his mind. It lifted only at brief intervals during the fifteen years that elapsed before death released him." Ritz ended his days in a clinic at Kusnacht near Lucerne and died there – in his native Switzerland – shortly after his son René and just at the end of the Great War that signalled the dissolution of the Belle Epoque which he had served so well.

The name of Ritz, however, lived on. Even though his own connection with the Ritz Hotel in London (opened 1906) was one in name only, César's illness did not mean that the standards of food, service and decor associated with his name were in any way lowered. His loyal colleagues upheld these important traditions. As far as the visual appearance of the hotel's interiors were concerned, Ritz's withdrawal meant that Charles Mewès and his new London partner, Arthur J. Davis, had an entirely free hand. When Mewès brought his ideas to Ritz, the ailing king of hoteliers could only repeat wearily, "Do what you like" – a pitiful contrast with the man who a few years before had concerned himself with every detail of his hotels.

The London Ritz in Piccadilly has been regarded as an architectural masterpiece from the day it was finished. It delights the social historian as a perfectly preserved survival of the Belle Epoque, and also the architectural historian as a beautiful construction, uniting with refinement and elegance such apparently disparate elements as its revolutionary steel frame and its Louis XVI-inspired ornamentation.

Flushed with the success of the various Ritz enterprises, one of César's London backers, William Harris, sought to take advantage of the magic name by setting up "The Ritz Hotels Development Company Limited" to exploit César Ritz's ideas all over the world. This was simply a managing and operating concern; it did not finance construction (that basic element had to be provided by local capital), but it offered the name, the managers, the good will, the patrons and forms of mutual advertising. Various agreements were drawn up with the sick César and his wife: in 1909, for instance, the couple gave "to the company the exclusive right of the use of the name of Ritz in connection with Hotels Restaurants and other similar establishments for the whole Continent of North America and Spain and will not be either directly or indirectly connected with or interested in any similar enterprises in North America or Spain without the consent of the Company."

Mewès participated in the design of the Ritz in Madrid – a Belle Epoque monument to the aspirations of King Alfonso XIII, who was determined that his capital should boast an hotel equal to the best in London and Paris. The Madrid Ritz opened in 1910, as did the Ritz-Carlton Hotel on Madison Avenue in New York City under the management of César Ritz's protégé, Albert Keller. Other Ritz Hotels followed in Lucerne, Buenos Aires, Mentone, Evian (two), Rome (two), Lisbon, Naples, Barcelona, Salsomaggiore, Montreal, and even Atlantic City. It has, as things have turned out, been impossible to protect the name from copyright. However vulgarized, as the label for all sorts of unlikely establishments and products, the word "Ritz" has never lost its *cachet*. Today perhaps half-a-dozen Ritz Hotels live up to the great traditions of César: those in Barcelona, Boston, Lisbon, London, Madrid and Paris, but there is no argument that the latter is *the* Ritz.

4. THE BELLE EPOQUE

Within months of the opening in Paris, royal visitors were visiting the Ritz like migratory birds. At the time when César had left the Savoy, the Prince of Wales was reported to have said, "Where Ritz goes, I go." He was true to his word and abandoned the Hôtel Bristol for the Ritz. The Tsar of Russia stayed there, and the Shah of Persia. The hotel also made its mark quickly as the fashionable place to dine. Boni de Castellane, who eventually married the American heiress Anna Gould and eagerly spent a large part of her fortune, told César that he was going to dismiss his own chef and entertain at the Ritz: "It is foolish to try to compete with you and Escoffier." Ritz's long-time patron Lady de Grey was particularly helpful in luring society to the handsome dining-room.

After placing his unmistakable stamp on the cuisine at the fledgling Ritz, Escoffier had moved on to the London Carlton in 1899. He was replaced in Paris by M. Gimon, formerly *chef de cuisine* at the Russian Embassy in Madrid, whose expertise in such Russian delicacies as *borscht*, *bliny* and *bitoky* was in demand with the flocks of Grand Dukes who frequented the hotel in those pre-Revolution days. They included the Grand Dukes Paul, Vladimir and Alexis, as well as Grand Duke Michael and Countess Torby; but anarchy and assassination were in the air. "No wonder," said Mme Ritz, "that when the Grand Dukes stopped at the Hotel Ritz the place was guarded like a fortress!"

The fare served up at the Ritz in this period reflects the style and extravagance of the Belle Epoque. The Maharajah of Kapurthala was clearly a lavish host, who treated his guests to Grande Fine Champagne Ritz 1800 to chase down the Château-Yquem 1877, Château Ducru-Beaucaillon 1875, and a magnum of Moet & Chandon 1889 for good measure. His menus were hand-coloured with Indian scenery and his coat of arms.

The menus for the great Exposition Universelle of 1900 are jokingly captioned "From the Equator . . . to the North Pole . . . And Back to the Ritz", with drawings by Lucien Hermond. For the covers of the Christmas and New Year *Reveillon* menus, 18th-century scenes were contrasted with those of the young 20th century; one year Papa Noël floated in a balloon above the Place Vendôme. The entertainers ranged from M. and Mme Depas performing *La Revue des Snobs* to Miss Celia singing "Kiss Kiss" ("*Chanson Américaine*"), from the Comédie-Française to Lewis Douglas ("American excentric [*sic*] dancer *des Folies Bergère*").

More periodic background is provided by the hotel's house magazine, *The Ritz Monthly*, which kept its readers abreast of "gossip, exhibitions, sport, decorative art, automobile world, entertainments, fashions", etc. These old publications contain such items as a report of an unseemly riot at Longchamp, when the "mob" wrecked the

Four eminent men personifying the Belle Epoque period of the Ritz: King Edward VII, one of César Ritz's earliest and most faithful patrons; the super-rich Maharajah of Kapurthala; Baron Henri de Rothschild; and Count Boni de Castellane, a leader of French society.

course after a false start to a race; notes on "French elegance" as still personified by Robert de Montesquiou, Boni de Castellane and other dandies; notices of Sarah Bernhardt's performances; and examples of Escoffier's menus.

In February 1907 *The Ritz Monthly* had a scoop for its in-house readers when the "Duke and Duchess of Lancaster" (otherwise King Edward VII and Queen Alexandra), who were staying in Paris "incognito" (though with a contingent of courtiers), gave a lunch at the Ritz for the Marquis and Marquise de Breteuil. The magazine's reporter effusively described a "centrepiece of *mauve* orchids, surrounded by bunches of Parma violets, intersected by hybrid orchids of the most delicate hues", though he claimed that he was unable to do justice to the beautiful floral decorations. As to the food, "The King deigned to express satisfaction to the Manager of the Ritz with regard to the execution of the menu, which had been ordered by His Majesty."

After coffee, Their Majesties and guests retired to the Louis XV Salon, "where King Edward had a somewhat lengthy conversation with the Marquis de Breteuil". The gossip columnist of *The Ritz Monthly* explained why the French had so much affection for the British monarch:

One of the characteristics of the King which particularly pleases the Republican Parisians is the simple manner in which he drops into a theatre with two or three gentlemen and enjoys the play as much as any boulevardier. That visit with the Queen to a circus was a charming surprise to the whole city; and whether it was a diplomatic move or not, Her Majesty laughed heartily at the clown's jokes.

The King was also responsible for a sordid contretemps in which the hotel featured prominently: the Countess of Warwick's attempt to blackmail the Royal Family over her affair with Edward VII. It was at the Ritz, in the suite of the royal "go-between" Arthur Du Cros, M.P., that Lady Warwick and her "agent", the notorious Frank Harris, met to thrash out their negotiations concerning letters from King Edward which began "My darling Daisy". In his biography of the erratic beauty and philanthropist under that title, Theo Lang described this curious conference as "surely the most outrageous one ever conducted under the luxurious roof of the Ritz".

According to Baroness de Stoeckl, in her memoirs of Belle Epoque Paris, "Then there were masked balls at the Opera, racing at Longchamp and Auteuil, teas at the Ritz, dress shows, flirtations and scandals; *au fond* life was so fast that the latter caused little stir or flutter." *Le Fif O'Clock* at the Ritz, an import from London, had swiftly become an institution; ladies of impeccable background were to be seen among the mirrors and flower arrangements of the *salon de thé* sipping tea from expensive porcelain and indulging in an occasional meringue or bonbon.

The great Australian soprano Nellie Melba was a patron of César Ritz, first at the Savoy in London and then at the Ritz Hotel itself. It was for her that Escoffier created Melba toast and Pêche Melba. *Overleaf:* the Place Vendôme and the Ritz Hotel as the scene of a State occasion in the mid-1930s.

By the turn of the century, the term *tout Paris* no longer applied only to the natives of that city, and the Ritz, in particular, was a second home to the numerous American expatriates who had settled in the capital. The millionairess Kate Moore (summed up as "large, affable, generous" in Mme Ritz's description of the 1898 opening) was prominent among them. An inveterate social climber who used to fill thirty *loges* at the Opéra with her "friends" every night of the season, Kate Moore was aptly called a "kind, silly woman" and "not a little absurd" by Cornelia Otis Skinner in *Elegant Wits and Grand Horizontals*. When she died, she made lavish bequests to those who had been helpful to her in her tireless quest for social acceptance. "Mrs Moore," commented Robert de Montesquiou, "has departed this life as she would from the Ritz, handing out tips."

RW
RW

5. THE FIRST WORLD WAR

From 1902 until his death in 1918, César Ritz took virtually no part in the running of his hotel. The management passed with no evident opposition or doubts to his immensely capable wife. Coming as she did from a family of hoteliers, and having participated in the planning of the Ritz, as well as in the early years when its foundations were being solidified, Marie-Louise had a strong influence on important decisions. Like César, she was a perfectionist; throughout her life she was known for the seriousness with which she took her responsibilities and for the severity of her judgment. An immaculately dressed and coiffed woman who lived till 1961, she made a top-to-bottom inspection of the hotel every day, followed along the corridors by her two Belgian griffons.

In the years just before the outbreak of the First World War, the hotel was enlarged by the extension into two other adjacent properties: the Rue Cambon house at the back and No. 17 Place Vendôme next door. This entailed greater responsibilities, but Marie-Louise was able to rely on a devoted, superbly trained staff whose principals had all been chosen by her husband.

The War itself, when it came, was obviously felt in various ways at the Ritz. The hotel offered one of its floors on the Place Vendôme side as a hospital for wounded officers. When those rooms were all occupied, the Cambon side became a hospital as well, and the smell of its disinfectants threatened to overpower the perfumes of the guests, whose numbers were greatly reduced.

In place of balls, there were charitable bazaars. The best tables in the dining-room were held not for royalty but for uniformed officers. Women of the aristocracy, without servants or coal to heat their salons, gave up their weekly "days" and turned to the hotels, principal among them the Ritz, which in addition to its central location always managed to be well heated. "For them, so far, hotels had been places to stay during holidays and, anywhere else, synonyms of sin," wrote Edmonde Charles-Roux, a one-time editor of *Vogue*. "Left to themselves, lonely wives dared to appear at the Ritz without the permission of their husbands. They went into the bar, a place which had been completely forbidden to them before the war. A lady could speak directly to a barman; she could brush shoulders with an atheist-politician; she could sit next to a parvenu and witness a discussion between speculators. This was entirely new."

On the night of the first major Gotha raid on Paris in July 1917, Marcel Proust and Jean Cocteau were dining at the Ritz with Paul Morand and Princess Soutzo. A hypnotist was hired to entertain the party and Princess Murat asked this entertainer whether he could cure her of grinding her teeth ("modest request," commented Proust); but she rather unkindly began to "come round" of her own accord while the hypnotist struggled through the appropriate gestures to get there first. Amid the general hilarity, the wail of the siren on the Eiffel Tower was suddenly heard. "Someone's trodden on the Eiffel Tower's toe, it's complaining," quipped Cocteau, but the air raid was about to begin. For more than an hour Proust stood on the balcony watching Paris lit up by the constellations of conflict.

In his account of that night, Proust compared the apocalyptic scene to El Greco's *Burial of Count d'Orgaz*, in which the events of heaven and earth are presented on two separate planes. The Ritz, or "earth", was notable for the sight of anxious ladies in nightgowns wandering about, clutching their ropes of pearls to their bosoms, as in a Feydeau farce.

One night towards the end of the War Proust was dining at a table next to Winston Churchill, then Minister of Munitions. Churchill, who was about to enter his years of wandering in the political wilderness, was no stranger to the Ritz; in her diary for 22 May 1912 Lady Violet Bonham Carter recorded a more carefree visit.

We all left London Tuesday morning. Amusing station send-off scene – Margot, Mrs West, Lady Blanche Hozier, Edwin Montagu, Venetia, Master of Elibank, Bongie, Micky, etc. We rumbled off to Dover in a Pullman Car full of Cabinet boxes, newspapers, letters, flowers. Calm crossing in bright sunshine. I read "Imaginary Speeches" with Winston all the way to Calais (we both specially enjoyed the very good one by Lord Rosebery). Then train-de-luxe to Paris where we all turned out and had delicious hot baths at the Ritz and an ambrosial banquet at Voisin before re-embarking in our train . . .

Glimpses of the Ritz in wartime Paris occur in the diaries of Lady Violet's sister-in-law, Lady Cynthia Asquith, whose husband "Beb" (the former Prime Minister's second son) and her friend Lord Basil Blackwood spent some of their leaves from the Front in the hotel. "Beb wrote the most comic and pathetic letters appointing a rendezvous with him at the Ritz Hotel," Lady Cynthia noted before Christmas 1917.

Queen Marie of Rumania and two daughters in the garden of the Ritz Hotel in March 1919, when the Versailles Peace Conference was taking place. The Queen's party occupied twenty rooms.

The American novelist Edith Wharton found dining at the Ritz with her fellow Americans Nancy Astor and the Countess of Essex one wartime evening a "spectral" experience. Only four other tables were occupied, and a single ghostly waiter in a long apron shuffled up and down the "empty vistas" of the unheated dining-room. All the years she lived in France Edith Wharton evinced a strange antipathy towards the Ritz; "Ritzian" was a term of severe reproof when spoken by her. This was such a well-known eccentricity in her circle that one of her friends divided the Paris ladies of his acquaintance into two classes: "Ritz vs. Anti-Ritz. The Anti-Ritz class contains only Mrs Edith Wharton." She was no happier when the Ritz enjoyed a resurgence as the popular and crowded meeting place for Allied officers. "I can't stand that scene of khaki and champagne," she told Henry James. When James asked whether there was some sort of rift betwen her and her special friend Walter Berry, who spent much of his time in the hotel, Mrs Wharton replied: "It is not a little rift but a little Ritz that's between us just now."

Queen Victoria's favourite son, the Duke of Connaught (a frequent guest at the Ritz), was staying in the hotel during one of the severest air raids of the War, but Mme Ritz told a journalist on *The Sphere* that "it did not disturb him at all". Although a good deal of glass was broken when bombs fell on the Place Vendôme, the Ritz survived the War with surprisingly few scars. This was all the more remarkable because the Prussian General von Kluck, who led the offensive against Paris, had a specific animus against the hotel. During the summer of 1914 before the outbreak of hostilities the dining-room of the Ritz was crowded every night. On one occasion a self-important figure accosted the *maître d'hotel* Olivier and demanded a table. Olivier, who had filled every available inch of space with extra tables, was unable to comply. This incensed the man; "But I am General von Kluck," he announced. Olivier offered a polite but mild apology; whereupon the Prussian turned on his heel and marched furiously out of the hotel. "For a moment I was afraid he was going to make trouble," said Olivier to one of his waiters.

Even the German General Alexander von Kluck was unable to intimidate Olivier Dabescat, the *maître d'hotel* who ruled at the Ritz like a benevolent dragon for some sixty years.

During the War Olivier, choosing not to observe the absurd rule that Allied officers on leave in Paris were not to be served alcohol, dispensed whisky and champagne from teapots. When the gendarmerie learned of this and served a summons on him, Olivier appealed to his friend and long-time Ritz resident Georges Mandel, Clemenceau's faithful supporter. In Olivier's presence, Mandel telephoned the gendarmerie: "*Annulez cette plainte, s'il vous plaît*," he said. And no more was heard of that.

For most of the War, the hotel managed to operate, if on a greatly reduced basis; for eight months it was shut down altogether, except for those portions assigned to the wounded. The only physical damage it suffered was the broken glass caused by the concussions from bombs dropped on the Place Vendôme.

Although 1918 brought the Armistice and rejoicing in victory, it was a year of deep private grief for Marie-Louise Ritz. Not only did René die early in the year at the age of 21, but in October, just weeks before the German capitulation, César Ritz finally died. A great sadness filled the hotel, but Marie-Louise's characteristic response after the funeral in Switzerland was to plunge herself even more deeply into the affairs of the Ritz, which by now had become her home – and, in effect, her life, as it would continue to be for many years to come.

6. THE TWENTIES

The Ritz recovered quickly after the War, retaining the loyalty of its pre-War clientele as well as attracting a new generation of high livers and big spenders. Mme Ritz was running the hotel, with the supremely able support of Victor Rey, another young Swiss who had enjoyed not only César's training but also his example. Resourceful, diligent and devoted to serving the guests' needs and caprices, Rey smoothly took over the post of manager from Henry Elles.

The American-born Dolly sisters were top entertainers in dance-mad Paris in the 1920s and were frequently seen being wined and dined at the Ritz by their various admirers.

Even before the Armistice, a young ambitious socialite like Henry ("Chips") Channon was calling the Ritz "the centre of all that the pre-war epoch had left". He recorded in his voluminous diary his impressions of dinner with Proust and Cocteau at the Ritz:

Their manners, usually so bad, were excellent tonight, and they seemed to compete as to which could be the more engaging. I felt stupid between the two wittiest men in Europe, drenched in a Niagara of epigrams. Jean is a stylist and his conversation is full of fire and rapier thrusts. He is like some faun that is indulged too long. He is haggard at 26, and his figure and smile have something mythological, something of the centaur in them.

Proust is quieter, longer-winded and more meticulous. His blood-shot eyes shine feverishly, as he pours out ceaseless spite and venom about the great. His foibles are Ruskin, genealogy and heraldry. He knows the arms and quarterings of every duke in Europe. His black hair was tidily arranged, but his linen was grubby, and the rich studs and links had been clumsily put in by dirty fingers.

Proust has always been kind to me, and I don't like to libel him in the pages of my diary, so I will boil down to the minimum all the rumours about him: that he loathes daylight and is called at tea-time, all the world knows. Does the world know that he tips with thousand franc notes, and that he has prolonged evening gossips with the Figaro coiffeur at the Ritz? With questionable taste, I asked him if it was true at dinner, and he nodded.

Proust also made a considerable impact on the British Ambassador, the 17th Earl of Derby, who said, "Of all the impressions my wife and I took home with us from Paris, Monsieur Proust was the most indelible. Yes, he was the first chap we'd ever seen dining in a fur-coat."

Harold Nicolson, as a young diplomat taking part in the Versailles Peace Conference of 1919, met Proust at the Ritz with Princess Soutzo. He noted in his diary that Proust was

white, unshaven, grubby, slip-faced. He puts his fur coat on afterwards and sits hunched there in white kid gloves. Two cups of black coffee he has, with chunks of sugar. Yet in his talk there is no affectation. He asks me questions. Will I please tell him how the committees work? I say, 'Well, we generally meet at 10.00, there are secretaries behind . . .' 'Mais non, mais non, vous allez trop vite. Recommencez.

Vous prenez la voiture de la Délégation. Vous descendez au Quai d'Orsay. Vous montez l'escalier. Vous entrez dans la Salle. Et alors? Précisez, mon cher, précisez.' So I tell him everything. The sham cordiality of it all: the handshakes: the maps: the rustle of papers: the tea in the next room: the macaroons. He listens enthralled, interrupting from time to time – "Mais précisez, mon cher monsieur, n'allez pas trop vite."

For the novelist Marcel Proust the Ritz was both a social venue and a haven. In the glittering dining-room he could observe and hobnob with the leading lights of international society. And in the room upstairs which was always reserved for him, this eccentric and hypersensitive chronicler of French life could escape from the very world he was so busy dissecting in his brilliant, tortuous style.

A few weeks later Nicolson met Proust again and afterwards made this note of the incident:

Dine with Jean de Gaigneron at the Ritz, Gladys Deacon there. Very Attic. Also Marcel Proust. Very Hebrew. Sit next to him. He asks more questions. I am amused by this. I suggest to him that the passion for detail is a sign of the literary temperament. This hurts his feelings. He says 'Non pas!' quite abruptly and then blows a sort of adulatory kiss across the table at Gladys Deacon.

In January 1922, the year he was to die, Proust came to the annual Ritz Ball where he watched demonstrations of the latest dance crazes and was introduced to the harpsichordist Wanda Landowska. According to the authoritative George Painter, he soon fled to his private room upstairs and "devoured a leg of lamb". Henry Elles, when he was hotel manager, had arranged this private room for Proust so that he could dine there at any time of night. The room in darkness, he would sit surrounded by waiters whom he had taught to work the light switches, the positions of which he knew by heart. The staff of the Ritz were enormously impressed and proud when Proust became famous as the author of *A la Recherche du Temps Perdu* and would search the newspapers for references to him. "The *Corriere della Sera*," recited Vespis, the Italian headwaiter in the Cambon Grill Room, "say Monsieur Proust's books are verra verra tiring, you must climb, climb, always, but it's worth while, because you see so far from the top!" Vespis was to die not long after this announcement: "poor Vespis," wrote Proust, "or happy Vespis, according to how you look at it – he's dead – is that a happy event? I don't know."

Proust was to find out soon enough. Even on his deathbed the Ritz remained an essential part of his life. "Can someone run and get me a peach or an apricot from the Ritz?" he asked; and, then, on the morning of 18 November 1922, he sent his driver Odilon to the Ritz for iced beer, predicting gloomily that, "like everything else, it will come too late." But Odilon returned to hear Proust murmur his all but final words: "Thank you, my dear Odilon, for fetching the beer."

Proust is best described by his friend Olivier of the Ritz. "He exacted the most absolute courtesy," Olivier told the art dealer René Gimpel, "in spite of the fact that he was able to come down to everyone's level and could put the humblest person at ease. He was extraordinarly sensitive; one evening, for example, he arrived at the very moment when an elevator was going off duty and the man did not altogether hide his ill-humour. This put Marcel Proust in a wild rage; but when I asked him if he wanted me to dismiss the man, he was firmly against it. He wouldn't even hear of his being suspended for two days, when I wanted to chastise him in this way."

Harold Nicolson had a very high opinion of the omnipotent Olivier, praising the way he blended with "a masterly precision the servile and the protective, the deferential and the condescending". But on one occasion, as Nicolson bore painful witness, Olivier's phenomenal memory failed him. The young diplomat agreed to lunch with the couturier Captain Edward Molyneux, whom he had met in the Rue de Rivoli; but "Only," said Nicolson, "if we go to the Ritz. Olivier is the only headwaiter who knows me, and I enjoy that." As they entered the dining-room, Olivier greeted Molyneux

("Bonjour, mon capitaine, Comment allez-vous?"), but to Nicolson he said with his habitual aplomb, "Mr Bonstetten, is it not?"

A well-known relic of the Belle Epoque who deserves a place in the pantheon of what Bernard Berenson once called "Ritzonia" is Liane de Pougy, the celebrated courtesan who attended the opening night in 1898 and was still going strong in the 1920s. In her notebook she mused on 14 May 1926, "I like the Ritz. It's a place where I find dear old friends from the past again . . ." Later "the nation's Liane" (unlike the other great courtesans of the period she was not a foreigner) fulfilled her ambition of becoming a nun.

In *Some People*, Harold Nicolson recounts amusing incidents concerning Arketall, Lord Curzon's valet. This somewhat alcoholic gentleman's gentleman attended Curzon while at the Ritz and one day forgot his Lordship's foot-rest, needed for an early morning departure to Lausanne; when he finally fetched it he tripped and shot down the curving staircase directly into Nicolson, with his feet in the air and the foot-rest held above his head. As he and Nicolson watched Curzon depart in his train, Arketall suddenly confided, "Ay left me 'at behind." Nicolson had a shaming recollection of "that disgraceful bowler lying on the Ritz stair carpet. They might even think it was le chapeau de Lord Curzon!" They were saved, however, from this embarrassment: a secretary joined them carrying a bowler. "They threw this into our motor as we were leaving the Ritz," she said.

Lord Curzon's second wife, the beautiful American heiress Grace Duggan who had been brought up in Argentina, was a "regular" at the Ritz. On 15 May 1922 she wrote,

I found the usual flowers awaiting me from M. de Castellane, Aga Khan, and Charles Mendl. I dined downstairs with Alfred [Duggan, her brother, who became a successful historical novelist late in life] – the usual Sunday crowd. Lots of people came to talk to me – Mr and Mrs Vansittart (he is looking much better and tells me he is in the doctor's hands here), Maggie Greville, Mrs Loeffler, Mendl and Castellane. I came to bed early and left Alfred downstairs to dance a little. My rooms are nice but noisy as they look on the Place Vendôme . . .

The next day "The Ritz was crowded for luncheon. I saw King Manoel of Portugal, Prince and Princess Christopher of Greece, the Duke of Portland, Bell Herbert, the Duchess of Roxburghe, and lots of Americans." During a visit later in the year she was happy to have her "old comfy rooms in the courtyard" though she was again displeased by the number of her compatriots: "The Hotel is very full, full of rather uninteresting Americans."

Lady Curzon certainly did not include among the latter her friend Elsie de Wolfe, the American wife of Sir Charles Mendl (who was press attaché at the British Embassy in Paris between the wars). For this pioneering interior decorator, who contributed to the making of Sutton Place as one of the most fashionable addresses in New York, the Ritz was a second home. A former actress, Lady Mendl was an inveterate hostess. Her various stunts included dyeing her hair green, learning to stand on her head at the age of 50 and throwing a lavish "Gold Ball" at the Ritz in the middle of the Depression.

She is supposed to have said to an ample woman at the Ritz, "Aren't you Elsa Maxwell, the woman who sings those *risqué* songs?"

"I'm Elsa Maxwell," this by no means ordinary personality replied. "But off-colour songs are not my stock-in-trade."

All the same, Maxwell performed some of Cole Porter's "secret" songs at a tea-party Lady Mendl gave at her "Trianon" villa in Versailles to a startled audience that included the then British Foreign Secretary, Arthur Balfour. As Elsa related in her uninhibited memoirs, *I Married the World*, she took the opportunity to invite Balfour to a dinner-party at the Ritz, to include the likes of Mrs Keppel, Princess Edmond de Polignac, Lord D'Abernon, Lady Ripon (formerly Lady de Grey), Grand Duke Alexander, Boni de Castellane and Sir Ronald Storrs. At the end of the dinner Balfour said: "My dear Miss Maxwell, allow me to thank you for the most delightful and degrading evening I have ever spent."

George Bernard Shaw is said to have remarked that Maxwell must be "the eighth wonder of the world" when he heard that she had refused a $5,000 Cartier jewel as a place-card for a dinner given in her honour at the Ritz, in preference for having the violinist Fritz Kreisler play for her.

But her parties were legendary, and certainly encapsulated the rapturous carelessness of the 1920s. She gave one at the Ritz for Jay O'Brien that cost around $20,000. O'Brien, an ex-chorus boy who had struck it rich by marrying the divorced wife of an heir to the Fleischman yeast fortune, asked Cole Porter what sort of present he could give Elsa for her birthday. Porter's answer was a party. Elsa thereupon commissioned Diaghilev's Ballets Russes to perform in the garden of the Ritz and invited 300 guests.

Among other figures of the period who were associated with the Ritz was Anita Loos, for whom Walter Berry gave a special lunch in honour of her classic Twenties novel *Gentlemen Prefer Blondes*. Even Edith Wharton overcame her dislike of the Ritz to meet the admired author, described by Frank Crowninshield of *Vanity Fair* as perhaps the smartest and certainly one of the prettiest women on earth. Miss Loos's famous book retails the amatory adventures of Lorelei Lee from Little Rock who moves from one Ritz Hotel to another.

From the 1920s on, the names associated with the Ritz began to have a more familiar ring than those of the earliest period: Scott Fitzgerald, Valentino, Pickford, Chanel, Woolworth, Rockefeller, the couple the world came to know as the Windsors – the roll call is virtually endless.

Year after year, while the post-war boom lasted, the Americans would begin to appear in Paris in May and be gone by October. Then the British would come, staying for a few days before leaving on the Blue Train for the Riviera. In the summers, clients would arrive for the season, bringing a dozen or more steamer trunks, which would sit in the corridors outside their suites. The women changed their costumes at least three times a day, for luncheon, tea and dinner; and often remained in the hotel for several days at a time without venturing out.

When the Americans departed in the autumn, they booked the same suites for the next year, and were assured of the services of the same maids and valets. The most affluent brought their own valets, maids and even chauffeurs, who were looked after by a special hotel staff. One veteran remembers a time when eighty such servants were in residence.

Aside from the attractions of Paris as a lively and enchanting centre of social and cultural activity, the advent of Prohibition in the United States gave Americans an additional incentive to spend as much time as they could in a city where alcohol not only flowed without hindrance but was also relatively inexpensive. The Cambon Bar accordingly became a true Mecca for visitors from overseas. Opened in 1921, and remodeled in 1936 by Jean Pascaud to incorporate the newest clean-cut Art Deco style, it was managed from its inception until 1947 (when he died) by Frank Meier, who played a large part in making it so popular. He was the sort of barman who remembered all his clients' whims, who was a real expert at mixing cocktails, and who would lend a willing ear to his habitués' tales of success or failure.

In those early days of the Ritz Bar, Cole Porter was one of the most consistent regulars. He spent something like nine hours a day there, less for the drink than for the ambience. He found it a good place to work, and was supposed to have composed "Begin the Beguine" at his favourite table.

Scott Fitzgerald was certainly a familiar face in the Bar, indeed something of a troublemaker. Frank Meier's assistant, Georges Scheuer, remembered an occasion when the writer was in the Bar and, for no self-evident reason, suddenly smashed a stranger's hat. He was warned that he would not be served if anything of that sort happened again, but it was impossible to pin Fitzgerald down to any promises when he was on one of his famous drinking binges.

In the carefree period of his early success, F. Scott Fitzgerald and his wife Zelda were frequent visitors at the Ritz. He in particular was an habitué of the Cambon Bar; his antics there have become legendary.

Another time, he was having a farewell drink before catching a boat at Le Havre and Georges called one of the taxis which were always available at the Rue Cambon entrance. It was the last time the driver, old Charles, was ever seen in Paris, for Fitzgerald not only had Charles drive him and the unruly Zelda all the way to Le Havre but, when they reached the pier, he decided on the spur of the moment that Charles and his cab should accompany them across the Atlantic. Charles and the taxi evidently became part of the Fitzgerald household.

Ernest Hemingway, who was eventually to become the most famous patron of the Ritz Bar, was first brought there by Scott Fitzgerald though he was far too poor in the early 1920s to buy his own drinks. The Ritz figures in his first novel *The Sun Also Rises*; one of the characters speaks of having been to the Bar for a drink that day. Had she stayed for lunch? Of course not, she replies, it was too expensive.

The Ritz Bar was originally for men only, though there were stories of the actress Constance Bennett gatecrashing in male attire; the women were assigned what Lucius

SELIGMANN
SELIGMANN
HELLSTERN
HELLSTERN.
HELLSTERN
23 COTY 23
23
23

YANTORNY
YANTORNY
LINKE
MEUBLES D'ART
LINKE
Eliane
MODES
Eliane
ROBES
BOUCHERON
BOUCHERON
BOUCHERON
J. GAILLARD
PARIS
952-RE4

pp. 86-87: Place Vendôme in the 1930s.

Beebe described as "the dreadful smoke-filled cubicle . . . known as the Cambon Dog House", a former writing-room across the lobby. In 1936 this was turned into a new small bar ("Le Petit Bar"), which built up a considerable reputation of its own, particularly after the Second World War, and has come to be known as the Hemingway Bar.

In the days when the sexes were segregated, it was rumoured that Mme Ritz would take up a post in the tiny barber's shop next to the main bar, in order to eavesdrop on the Rabelaisian conversations of the male clients. In 1935, when she went over to London for the Silver Jubilee of King George V and Queen Mary, she told the London *Evening News*, "They became engaged under our roof," recalling those golden days of the Hôtel de Provence in Cannes.

Janet Flanner wrote in the *New Yorker* of Marie-Louise:

She came into the dining-room hatted, gloved and parasoled, although she was in her own home. Every male form rose from its chair a little as she passed. The gentlemen bowed. The more important waiters pushed the minor waiters behind them so that they themselves could make the deepest bow. She acknowledged the bows regally, yet one knew her eye was taking in everything everywhere.

Although Ernest Hemingway was evidently introduced to the Ritz by Scott Fitzgerald, it is Hemingway who established a more permanent association with the hotel. He and Charles Ritz particularly shared a deep love of fishing; here in the late 1950s Hemingway is seen at the annual dinner Charles Ritz (left) gave for his fishing friends. In 1985 the Hemingway connection was commemorated by the establishment of the Ritz Paris Hemingway Award, a prize of $50,000 given annually to the author of a distinguished novel published in the English language.

The Ritz probably experienced its most lavish prosperity in the late 1920s. It was in this period that Gulbenkian used the hotel as his Paris residence; when Barbara Hutton, the much-married Woolworth heiress, would arrive with seventy trunks for long stays; when one of the Vanderbilt women would be conveyed across the Place Vendôme every morning to deposit her pearl necklace in the safe of the Morgan Bank; when Lord Furness, president of the Suez Canal Company, would arrive from England with a selection of his home-grown orchids.

7. THE THIRTIES

The Wall Street Crash of 1929 brought that phase to a sudden end. Cancellations, first from America, and then from England, were the order of the day. The majority of those handsome and well-tended rooms were unrented. In the bar, survivors drank quietly and joylessly. Janet Flanner reported that "the pretty ladies have to pay for their cocktails themselves."

The burden of coping with this unsettling situation fell on the capable shoulders of Claude Auzello, who succeeded Victor Rey as managing director. Unlike his Swiss predecessors, Auzello was a Frenchman from Nice, a qualified lawyer who worked his way up from the bottom, became manager under Rey in 1925 and managing director in 1937. There was an obvious need in the Thirties to undertake economies in the

The Cambon Bar, once the exclusive domain of men, finally opened its Art Deco doors to women in 1936.

Douglas Fairbanks, Sr., athletic star of silent adventure motion pictures, relaxes on a couch in his suite at the Ritz.

running of the hotel; Auzello cut out the middleman suppliers and himself went to Les Halles at 5.30 a.m. three mornings a week to buy food. A strict disciplinarian, he was not easy on staff at the hotel who threatened to go on strike; he fired would-be troublemakers and worked behind the scenes to prevent a government bill that was designed to institute inflexible working hours in hotels. He was probably the right kind of man to run the Ritz in that uncertain period, but he did not arouse affection among his staff.

It was in this situation of adverse economic conditions and a dwindling clientele that Charles Ritz was induced to take a hand in running the hotel. Because of his American background he was despatched to the United States, where he visited twenty of the leading cities in thirty days, seeking to impress on travel agents and potential visitors that the Ritz had not been designed only for millionaires. In getting his message across to a Depression-stricken nation, he coined the phrase, "The Ritz is not ritzy." Up to that time the Ritz had never needed to beat its own drum.

Little by little, the situation improved. Some of the regulars ventured forth, the rooms began to be occupied again. Lady Mendl flouted the Depression with her famous Gold Ball. *Vogue* said of the Ritz in 1937: "At the heart of Paris, it seems to preside over the rhythms of the city."

In 1934 the most celebrated lady in the history of the hotel installed herself in a suite on the Vendôme side, Gabrielle ("Coco") Chanel, the couturière. A friend once said that it took six years to get Chanel from her office across the street into the Ritz for lunch, and then three hours to get her out. But once she moved in, the Ritz was to remain her only home in Paris for the rest of her life. She brought her furniture with her, setting up her Coromandel screens and created a personal setting for her new life. Her biographer Edmonde Charles-Roux wrote that "an undeniable wanderlust" had driven Coco away from the fashionable *faubourgs*; the attraction of the Ritz was that she had never lived there before.

The strikes of the late 1930s also affected the House of Chanel in the Rue Cambon, resulting in a picket line a few doors down from the hotel. The "workroom delegates" arrived at the front door of the Ritz, demanding of a doorman that "the boss" be informed of their presence. Mademoiselle sent word that she did not know what a "workroom delegate" was and that she would see nobody. She told the doorman she would go to No. 31 Rue Cambon, as she did every day, when she was ready.

"They might not let you in," said the doorman.

"We'll see about that," replied the unflappable couturière, who put on her trademark outfit, a navy-blue suit, with a big rope of pearls, in order to face the fray. "A

Opposite, Gabrielle Chanel, longtime resident of the Ritz whose *couturier* establishment was across from the Rue Cambon entrance to the hotel.

tremor ran through the Ritz," Mme Charles-Roux recounts. "Would *they*, or wouldn't *they*, let her in?" The answer was that they would not. The humiliation Coco felt left lasting scars. In 1939 she closed her workshops.

Within hours of the hotel's requisition by the Nazis after the fall of Paris in 1940, Chanel's suite was cleared of its contents. Not a refugee by nature, she returned to the capital in August 1940 to find herself without a base. She was determined to stay on at the Ritz and accepted "a scrappy little room" on the Rue Cambon side of the hotel. "What's the use of changing?" she said to friends. "Sooner or later all the hotels will be occupied. Then what? I may as well stay here. My room is too small? That will make it cheaper."

In the days when a great deal of weight was placed on decorum of dress, even so valued a guest of the Ritz as the Woolworth heiress, Barbara Hutton, ran into difficulties when she appeared at the hotel in shorts and bobby socks.

Mademoiselle, like the Ritz, was a survivor, though the Ritz was to emerge from the Second World War with considerably more credit than the couturière. "Coco Chanel," wrote David Pryce-Jones in *Paris in the Third Reich*, "was to hole up in the Ritz with an aristocratic German officer; she scarcely emerged from her ivory love nest except to go on a dubious mission to Spain, neither quite cocotte nor quite spy."

8. THE SECOND WORLD WAR

The dining-room in the late 1930s, its tables crammed as usual.

Overleaf: The Ritz survived the Second World War, but they were grim years. In this photograph, taken during the Occupation, two German soldiers are standing at the entrance.

On 10 June 1940, as the great French Army was disintegrating on all fronts and the roads to the south of Paris were clogged with panicked civilians, Hans Elmiger, resident manager of the Ritz Hotel, paid a call on Georges Mandel, the Minister of the Interior. Elmiger, a grandson of Col. Maximilian Pfyffer, the man who "discovered" César Ritz, had been working at the hotel since 1924; as a German-speaking Swiss, he had been deputized to deal with the Germans when they arrived in Paris. Mandel, a widower, had lived in Room 124 of the hotel since 1920; as a Jew, he had special reason to fear the Germans, and was about to quit Paris in any case to join the rest of the French government in Bordeaux. The brief discussion between these two men was to determine the fate of the Ritz during the four momentous years of the German occupation.

HOTEL
RITZ
RESTAURANT

Elmiger had come to seek Mandel's advice as to whether he should close the hotel or try to keep it open. Don't close down, Mandel said, because if you do the Germans will requisition the hotel in any case, whereas if you remain open, they will come as paying guests. Elmiger accepted the advice.

The decision to continue in operation reverberated through the hotel. Word was passed to the staff that Ritz standards should be maintained insofar as that was possible. A number of the staff, fearing that they might be impressed into forced labour, decided to flee. As a result, lift operators became concierges overnight, and pages manned the lifts.

On June 14th, at 7 a.m., a detachment of German motorcyclists rolled up to the entrance of the Ritz, followed by a group of officers armed with appropriate documents, letterheads, and information as to the number of clients (18) and staff (26) still in the hotel.

Late that evening, when the occupation of the Ritz was a *fait accompli*, a squad of war correspondents in the tow of a German officer descended on the premises in search of something to eat. Among them was Louis P. Lochner of the Associated Press who reported that the manager "almost had an apoplectic stroke" as he pleaded that the kitchen had already closed. Not to be denied, the German officer found a soldier who knew how to cook and sent him and some helpers to the kitchen. Five minutes later, four formally clad waiters suddenly appeared. "Where the manager picked them up we don't know," Lochner wrote, "but apparently it seemed like sacrilege to him to have army privates attempt to serve a meal in an exclusive hotel as though they were ladling food in any army soup kitchen."

As Mandel (who was in due course assassinated by the French Vichy militia) had predicted, the Germans came as paying guests, though the authorized room charges were paltry, and the bills, in any case, were passed on to the French government. Most noteworthy of the German "guests" was Hermann Goering, who arrived a week after the Germans had taken Paris. Hans Elmiger showed the portly field marshal to the Imperial Suite, whereupon Goering asked a favour: could Elmiger go to Guerlain on his behalf and obtain a perfume the German much admired? When Elmiger protested that he had no car, Goering volunteered his own staff car and driver. The store, it developed, was closed. "Don't worry, Herr Director," Goering replied after Elmiger had returned empty-handed, "I know how to get it opened."

Ironically, it was Elmiger who had attended to a special request from a recently departed, equally noteworthy occupant of the Imperial Suite. Winston Churchill had come to France to tour the Maginot Line before the French collapse. "Do you still have the same cuisine?" he asked Elmiger after being shown to his suite. "Certainly," Elmiger replied. "Then," said the British leader, "I would like to have a sole served to me for breakfast every morning, the way you make them at the Ritz."

Goering's reputed purpose in Paris was to take charge of the Luftwaffe's bombing assault on England, but he seemed to spend as much time pillaging French art collections. According to A.E. Hotchner, whose novel *The Man Who Lived at the Ritz* portrayed Goering, among others, the field marshal spent much of his time in his suite, consuming morphine pills, and often dressed in women's clothes. Elmiger recalls one occasion when Goering descended from the Imperial Suite swinging his marshal's baton – solid gold and studded with diamonds, made especially for him by Cartier – like a majorette. At the sight of him, a group of officers waiting for him burst into laughter.

The Germans used the Ritz to reward mostly high-ranking officers for meritorious service. During their leaves of absence from the front, they would be put up on the Place Vendôme side of the hotel, checking their arms just inside the entry. The Rue Cambon side, closed at first, eventually reopened to serve foreigners and French civilians.

The latter were severely criticized at the outset by their countrymen for living – even though segregated – in the same hotel with the enemy; eventually the criticism was muted by the realization that the Ritz guests were in a position to obtain information not otherwise available.

The tone of the staff had been set from the first by Claude Auzello, who by this point had become the acting managing director. After being demobilized in September 1940, Auzello returned to Paris from the south and vowed that while he would continue to run a hotel in which the Germans were housed, he would never shake hands with one of them. In the lobby one day, General Otto von Stulpnagel, in charge of German troops in Paris and a resident of the hotel, walked up to Auzello, his right arm outstretched. Auzello bowed, turned and departed.

Nothing happened to Auzello, apparently because von Stulpnagel understood his feelings. But a few years later Auzello's American wife, Blanche, was put into jail after being overheard denouncing the Nazis while dining at Maxim's. It was not discovered that she was Jewish, and she was eventually released.

Auzello attempted, without much success, to organize the hoteliers of Paris into a resistance group. He did manage to help set up a coding system, used mostly to place fictitious orders for food, by which employees of the hotel were able to pass along information on the location of key German personnel.

The occupation of the Ritz ended on 25 August 1944, the day the Allies entered Paris. It was long believed that Ernest Hemingway liberated the Ritz but the story told by his biographer Carlos Baker is somewhat less dramatic. Assigned to an American army unit as a correspondent for *Collier's*, Hemingway had taken an increasingly active role in the fighting as his unit approached Paris, using his excellent French to obtain valuable information on the location of the Germans and even engaging in reconnaissance with a group of irregulars who had coalesced around him. Although he had

Claude Auzello, as acting managing director, and Mme Ritz were able to keep the hotel alive during the war years.

made no secret of his desire and intention to liberate the Ritz, the hotel was his third stop in Paris on the 25th, after the Traveller's Club and the Café de la Paix. By the time he arrived, the Germans had gone, and it was the "imperturbable" Auzello who awaited him at the door. He immediately installed himself in his favourite haunt, the Cambon Bar – to which all the high-ranking Allied officers and beautiful women in Paris appeared to make their way before the day had ended.

The next day, as Hemingway was enjoying a brandy following lunch at the hotel with several correspondent friends, a member of the group, Helen Kirpatrick, announced that she was leaving in order to observe the victory parade. "Daughter," Hemingway said, "sit still and drink this good brandy. You can always watch parades but you'll never again celebrate the liberation of Paris at the Ritz."

9. AFTER THE WAR: CHARLES RITZ

Claude Auzello and the aged Mme César Ritz pulled the hotel together again as Paris struggled to regain normality, and it was not until 1953, when his mother was 85, that Charles Ritz replaced her as Chairman of the Board.

Charles Ritz was a hero to many people, not because he cast a heroic figure – in fact he was on the small side, and extremely lean – but because of the equanimity, grace and good humour with which he conducted his life in the face of great duress. He recognized very early in his life that he would have to spend most of it under the thumb of a domineering and powerful mother, about whose affections he was uncertain to begin with.

Charles Ritz exercising his casting arm with a champion fisherman, Cresevault, inside the hotel.

Overleaf, a scene from the film *Love in the Afternoon* starring Audrey Hepburn and Gary Cooper. With Charles Ritz's blessing, most of the scenes that took place in the Ritz were shot *in situ*.

What was most remarkable about him was that he lacked pretensions of any kind. As Chairman of the Board, he did not even maintain an office. He was uncomfortable

After the Second World War, American movie stars returned to the Ritz as regular visitors. *Above*, Gene Tierney with Aly Khan, who was once married to Rita Hayworth.

being addressed in a formal manner and tried – in vain, for the most part – to have members of the staff call him "Monsieur Charles".

For all the advantages available to him, Charles Ritz preferred to live simply. When his mother died in 1961 he moved to her suite, but soon abandoned it for less elaborate quarters. He slept in a small bed and, except for cleaning, kept his own room in order. He knew as much as the best *maître d'hotel* about food and wine, and would often order unforgettable meals for special clients or friends, but his own preferences at table were plebeian. His favourite dish, by far, was spaghetti, which he ate whenever he could.

On the surface, everything seemed in order as Charles took charge. The aura of the hotel was intact; the hotel's register contained the most prestigious names from several continents. But times were changing, a situation that became increasingly apparent as the Fifties drew to an end. As people took to air transport in increasing numbers, the nature and pace of travel assumed new perspectives. There seemed less reason to spend a week on a transatlantic crossing. Travellers would no longer arrive at the Ritz with numbers of steamer trunks, or servants to unpack them; they would no longer stay through the summer, or use the Ritz as headquarters for their European tours. Visits might be for no more than several days, a few weeks at the most; then it was time to move on to locations previously impractical or perhaps inaccessible.

Political and economic changes throughout the world were mirrored in the changing clientele. For a while after the Second World War, the British returned in gratifying numbers, sidestepping currency restrictions by borrowing francs from Georges Scheuer in the Cambon Bar, or Black Max Intrator, an Egyptian, and paying it back to their London bank accounts. But soon a certain Mr Tarr, a British detective, began showing up at the Cambon Bar, making notes of who was there. This was nothing more than a deterrent, but it emphasized the reality of Britain's difficult condition.

Many South American clients stopped coming, particularly Argentinians; so, after 1959, did the Cubans. Nor were the ranking families of Europe immune to the changing times. When the wedding reception of Prince Lobcowitz and Françoise de Bourbon-Parme took place at the Ritz in January 1960, with Habsburgs, Bonapartes and Braganzas present, and light sparkling off the diamond tiaras and elaborate decorations, it was for resident manager Janusz Zembrzuski more than an extraordinarily elegant sight; it was the end of an epoch.

Ritz thought so too. He read into all these changes portents of a fundamental change in tastes, a desire to modernize, streamline, simplify. But these were taboo words at the Ritz. There was an entrenched belief that clients patronized the hotel precisely because it had resisted the very changes he now sought to implement. In an article which appeared in the Paris *Herald-Tribune* in 1964, Mary Blume reported that Charles was regarded as the *enfant terrible* of the Ritz Hotel: "It was he who brought in a time clock, a potato-frying machine and dictaphones, and it was he who shocked people half his age [72] by creating the Espadon Grill and by redecorating the bar last year." He told Blume in an interview that he wanted to put electric toasters in each room, but it wasn't possible just yet. On the other hand, he had succeeded with the showers: "I hate little showers with small holes," he said, "so I decided that since Americans are the world's greatest shower-takers they must make the best showers. All our shower heads are imported from the United States and they are first-rate."

The Duke and Duchess of Windsor stayed at the Ritz for long periods after the Second World War.

Opposite, Monique Ritz, who managed the Ritz until it was sold in 1979.

Ritz's arrival appeared to place the greatest strain on Claude Auzello, the autocratic managing director. Ritz's desire for change was a challenge to the way Auzello had always done things.

Bit by bit, Auzello became ever more depressed. To add to his anxieties, his wife Blanche became seriously ill. On 29 May 1969, fearing that Blanche would not be able to care for herself, Auzello shot her to death and then killed himself.

In spite of this tragedy, and with the help of his wife Monique, Charles Ritz instituted a redecorating programme. But paint and furniture alone could not solve the problems inherent in a building whose origins dated to the 18th century, and whose plumbing and electricity had been installed before the turn of the 20th century. What had to be done would not happen in Charles Ritz's lifetime.

RITZ
15

10. THE RENAISSANCE OF THE RITZ

Upon the death of Charles Ritz in 1976, the leadership of the hotel once more passed to a woman. Like her husband and his father, Monique Ritz was Swiss, a Genevese, and like him, too, she had a nimble mind and a zest for life: her predilection was for athletics, at which she excelled. They had married in 1971, following a long liaison, when she was 48 and he 80.

When Monique Ritz took over, the hotel was supported by its reputation and little else. It was losing business to other hotels in the upper luxury class. Its prestige had begun to wane. Heroic measures were required, but they would be costly; the other stockholders in the company that had always owned the hotel, who included among others the wife of Sir Isaiah Berlin (the former Aline de Gunzbourg), Col. George

The Ritz reborn: here, the recently redecorated entrance hall fulfils César Ritz's wish to make the visitor feel as if he were in an elegant private home.

Malcolm of Poltalloch (a grandson of Lillie Langtry), certain Rothschild interests and Baron Hans Pfyffer d'Altishofen, were not in favour of additional investment, particularly of the magnitude required to correct the deficiencies that were now finally recognized in full.

Water pipes had rusted throughout the hotel, and were too small in any case to service all the rooms at the same time. The heating system was a combination of many systems improvised over the years; it functioned poorly, and sometimes failed. Transformers were underpowered and unreliable, the voltage too low to sustain modern appliances. Rugs and carpets needed replacing. Public rooms were due for redecorating. Most of the bathrooms, originally in tiles and ceramic, would have to be gutted before they could be modernized.

The Ritz was in fact losing money, a state of affairs that could not continue. As sentimental as the owners might feel about the hotel, they had to consider selling.

Through the years, there had been many inquiries – most of them from established hoteliers – as to whether the Ritz was for sale. When the new owners of the Paris Ritz were at last identified, it took everyone by surprise.

Mohamed, Salah and Ali Al Fayed are the sole owners of Alfayed Investment and Trust, a company that runs the brothers' investments in shipping, construction, real estate, banking and oil and, lately, hotels and department stores. Until their purchase of the Ritz in 1979, they had never bought a hotel, and the only one in their past was owned by their father when they were growing up in Egypt. Why, then, the Ritz – which, bought for $30 million, would require another $100 million for its renovation before the last penny was spent?

Three elements motivate collectors to acquire a work of art: the love of beauty; the prestige of ownership; and the possibility of appreciation. All three elements were

The Espadon Restaurant, on the Rue Cambon side of the hotel, was one of Charles Ritz's contributions and a very popular one at first. Revived in 1980 after years of decline it quickly attained the distinction of two rosettes in the Michelin guide.

present in the acquisition of the Ritz by the Al Fayed brothers – and a fourth element as well, the fulfilment of a fantasy. When Mohamed Al Fayed was a child, his parents took him to the Ritz on a holiday. He was so overwhelmed by the charm of the hotel that he promised himself to own it one day.

The Al Fayed brothers left Egypt in the mid-Fifties, after the overthrow of King Farouk and the assumption of power by Colonel Gamal Abdel Nasser. Raised by British nannies, educated in British schools and unabashed admirers of British history, traditions and ethics, they naturally gravitated to London after finishing their studies. Over the years, they gradually enlarged the family businesses into the financial empire that exists today. Published reports have put the worth of their holdings at £500 million or more. Although the Al Fayeds will not comment, it may well be considerably more. In 1984 and 1985 alone, they paid more than £800 million for the House of Fraser, the corporation that operates Harrod's in London; as usual, they did not just buy control, they bought 100 per cent of the stock – and without the help of the banks.

Of the three brothers, Mohamed is the acknowledged leader, but he minimizes his role. "I'm the boss, but only because I'm the eldest," he insists. "Either of the other two are perfectly capable of being the boss." Although their business activities – particularly their acquisition of the world's most famous hotel and then the world's most famous department store – have inevitably thrust them into the public consciousness, all three brothers are intensely private men. Even their awesome contributions to charity – they tithe themselves each year – have never been announced.

Because silence begets mystery, and mystery begets suspicion, the Al Fayeds' acquisition of the Ritz inevitably produced fear among lovers of the hotel that the brothers might permanently alter its character. That fear has proved to be totally unfounded.

The familiar garden on the Vendôme side has been brought up to date and regained its popularity in clement weather.

Overleaf, The dining-room redecorated, and a splendid display of fresh fish.

BLANC
Fils

The restoration of the Ritz has turned into a classic example of the classic French phrase: *Plus ça change, plus c'est la même chose.* "Everything has either been replaced, or will be replaced – and yet resembles its original image," says architect Bernard Gaucherel with appropriate pride.

The tradition and history of the hotel have been enshrined in the names of the many personalities associated with it. Proust, among the earliest clients who fell in love with the Ritz, is commemorated by the suite shown here. And overleaf is a photograph of the suite which bears Chanel's name, and which gives the impression that Coco has just stepped out for a minute.

Two views of the Proust Suite, one of several refurbished to commemorate particular personalities associated with the Ritz.

Les textiles de l'Inde

LE NOUVE
TRAIN BLE
VERS LA COTE
D'AZUR

Previous page: the sitting-room of the Scott Fitzgerald Suite.

On these and the following two pages are photographs of the stately Imperial Suite, which has accommodated not only crowned heads, Hermann Goering and Winston Churchill, but such celebrities as Henry Kissinger and Woody Allen.

One of Mr Al Fayed's first moves after the acquisition was to appoint the dynamic young *président de l'hôtel*, Frank Klein. A graduate in hotel management from Cornell University, Klein is only the hotel's sixth general manager, the successor to Henry Elles, Victor Rey, Claude Auzello, Janus Zembrzuski and Bernard Penché. Klein had served in various capacities at the Savoy and the Berkeley in London, the Ritz in Madrid, the Bar au Lac in Zurich, and came to Mohamed Al Fayed's attention when he was Resident Manager of the Hôtel Georges V in Paris. Klein too has played a significant role in bringing the Ritz up to date.

TELEX

Every room in the hotel, both public and private, has been redecorated. The heating system has been completely replaced. Air-conditioning has been installed throughout, the plumbing overhauled down to the last rusty pipe, with new fixtures in all the bathrooms, which have been refaced in marble. Huge modern generators have been installed in the hotel to furnish power in the event of emergencies. Instead of one underground floor, there are now three, housing a swimming pool, health club, squash court, *salon de nuit* for suppers and dancing, complete new kitchen and vastly improved facilities for the staff.

The bathrooms attached to suites or even to single bedrooms afford a pleasure difficult to define. Nothing has been overlooked in an effort to provide the maximum in practical comfort.

One of Mr Al Fayed's most charming achievements has been the creation of some twenty-two opulent suites; not only the restored Imperial Suite, on the first floor overlooking Place Vendôme, with its stately Empire furniture upholstered in a vibrant red satin, but also the Chopin Suite all in yellow, the Coco Chanel suite with its

PARIS
PARIS
PARIS

Previous pages:
The bedroom of the Chopin Suite manages to be both romantic and rather severely Empire at the same time.

Portraits of the Duchess and Duke of Windsor in the suite that bears their name.

mementoes of its original occupant, and those named after the Windsors, Proust and Cocteau. In the early years, the Imperial Suite was the temporary venue of many crowned heads, but it has also been occupied more recently by Richard Nixon, Gina Lollobrigida, Roger Moore, Woody Allen and Mia Farrow, Elton John, and Madonna.

In the last twenty years, the number of clients from the worlds of entertainment and fashion have showed the greatest increase; in our present world they are often the greatest earners and the greatest spenders. But the hotel still treasures its traditional clientèle, the "old faithfuls" who represent the strongest tradition of the Ritz. And the new facilities, which have been created through the recent reconstruction, attract a new, much younger, breed of business executives, who need and enjoy contemporary comforts and equipment, but also appreciate all that was best in the past. They agree with Mr Al Fayed when he claims to have rescued a precious heirloom from decay: "That's what I take great pride in – that I have preserved a national treasure."

pp. 138–143:
The Espadon Bar (formerly the Cambon Bar); two views of the Salon Psyché, one of the hotel's large banqueting rooms; at the end of the corridor on the sixth floor is a semicircular entry to one of the new suites.

Berthelot

By 1990, more than ten years after the Al Fayed family took it over, all the elements of the modernized, resurrected Ritz were finally in place. To this task, the new owners brought the same attention to detail and painstaking perfectionism as César Ritz had done at the outset. Now, as then, the unswerving aim was to cater to the desires of the clientèle, to create a sumptuous and luxurious background for people who expect and demand nothing but the best.

Mr Mohamed Al Fayed

Opposite: The richly carpeted corridor that links the Rue Cambon entrance with the Place Vendôme is one of the most famous and exclusive shopping malls in the world.

The three major innovations are the establishment of the Ecole de Gastronomie Française Ritz-Escoffier; the night club-discothèque, approached from the Rue Cambon side of the hotel; and the subterranean swimming pool-health club combination. Each of these has proven to be eminently successful, and caters to some degree to people outside the hotel as well as to the honoured guests. The night club, for instance, operates on a membership basis, but anyone staying in the hotel is automatically welcome. The cooking school caters largely to the general public and has attracted Americans, Japanese, and Europeans visiting Paris, including the Earl and Countess Spencer, father and stepmother of HRH the Princess of Wales, who attended one of the very first courses. The Health Club is perhaps most directly intended to serve the needs and wishes of the hotel's clients, and is appropriate to the admirable and widespread vogue for physical fitness.

CIVANYAN
COCON
H.CIVANYAN

The Ritz Health Club symbolizes the many changes that have been brought about by the new management, and it is happily in line with César Ritz's own ideas about health and hygiene. The opulent swimming pool (shown on the previous pages) is 16m x 7m and decorated in Greco-Roman style; its warm-toned frescoes and the wealth of columns lend a hint of ancient times. In combination with the jacuzzis (above), Turkish bath and sauna, it provides equipment and an atmosphere calculated to ease the body and mind after a long air journey or a long night out. (The wonderful space of the pool can also be used for public functions and exhibitions. Once the pool is covered, the whole area becomes a hall of splendid dimensions.)

Another important feature of the Health Club is the gymnasium (above right), where the client can not only enjoy a bracing game of squash but also have a workout under professional supervision. In the contemporary world of fitness-consciousness, such provisions play a large part in the choice of a couple or family as to what hotel they want to stay in. In their day, Scott Fitzgerald and Hemingway were certainly more interested in what the Cambon Bar had on offer, but today's travellers, who have to cope with the new dislocations and discomforts of jet travel, tend to be more appreciative of a session of body-building than a short-lived alcoholic pick-up. The Ritz Health Club would have gladdened César's heart!

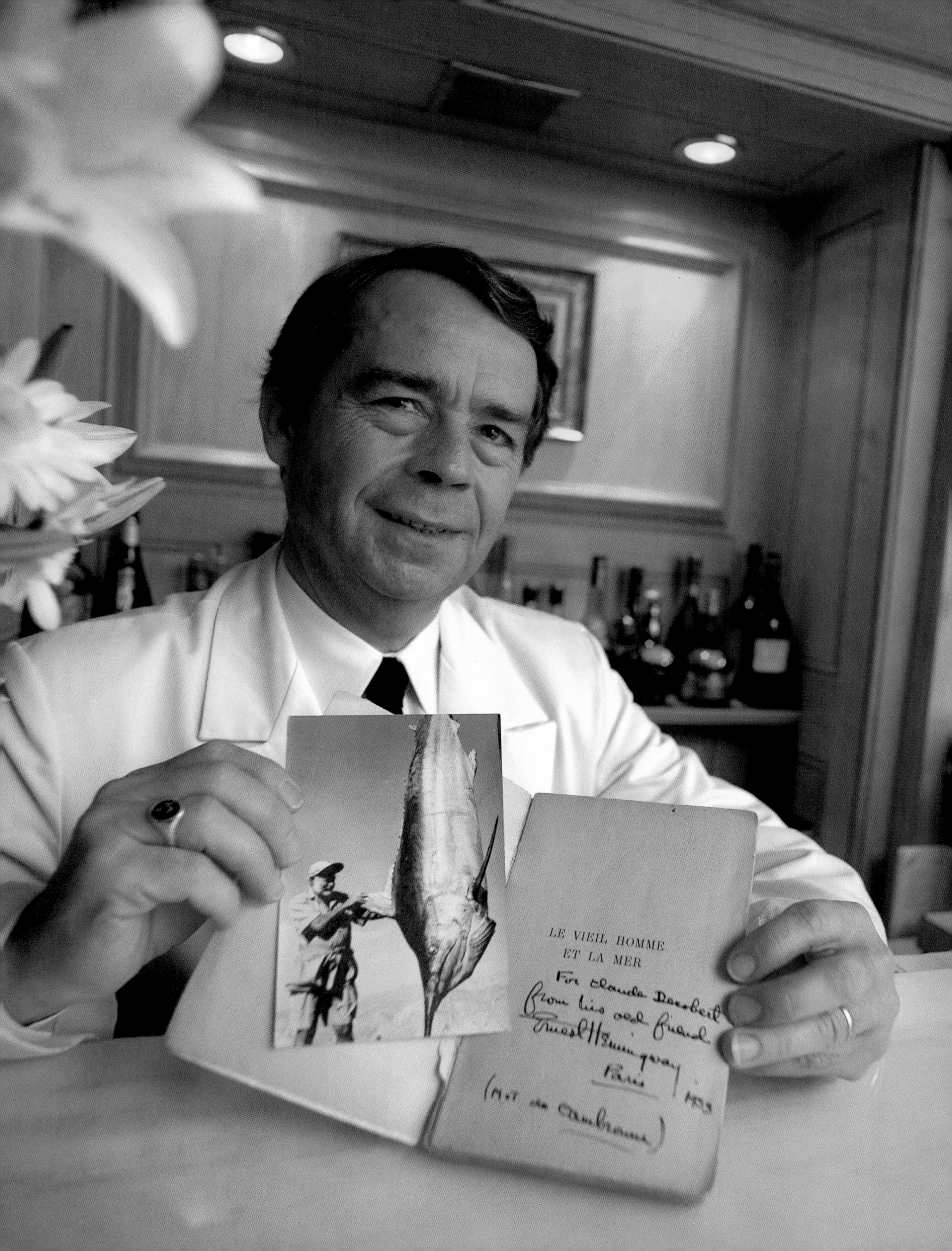
LE VIEIL HOMME
ET LA MER

As though guided by César Ritz's classic, nineteenth-century principle that the ultimate test of a hotel was its cuisine, the new management plucked two stars from the French restaurant firmament as part of its programme to remake the Ritz. The first of these was Guy Legay, chef of the highly respected restaurant Ledoyen, to be director of cuisine for the entire hotel. The second was Franco Gentileschi, *maître d'hôtel* at Maxim's, who was appointed director of the L'Espadon Restaurant.

Gentileschi's first order of business was to restore the kind of service that existed in the best restaurants of France twenty and thirty years ago, before changing styles led to relaxed standards. He wants a return to an elegance of the past. As to his tastes in food, they are classic, too; he detests – his word – *nouvelle cuisine*.

Legay seems by comparison both more contemporary and more eclectic. He is intent on avoiding a rich cuisine. "Cuisine ought to be transparent," he says. "You shouldn't mask the ingredients, it is like couture. If a dress is very simple, one can see the beauty. If there are a lot of ruffles you can cover up the mistakes underneath."

In his kitchen, Legay's primary responsibility is to create new dishes. "The ideas are mine, I perfect them with my subordinates and teach them how to do the dish. My principal function is to make sure the cuisine gets done." If he does not make concessions to undeveloped palates, he does try to respond to the tastes of his more discerning clients. "The success of a chef is being able to adapt the kitchen to the customers. I have clientèle from all over the world at the Ritz. I'd be foolish not to listen to them."

The cellars of the Ritz – one of 30,000 bottles in the hotel, another of 100,000 bottles in a 15th-arrondissement warehouse – are steeped in history. When César Ritz created his hotel, he bought large reserves of brandy and port. Some of these bottles are still in the cellars, the brandies dating back to 1812, the ports to the 1840s. The wines date back to 1897, and include the famous vintage years of 1928, 1929, 1947, 1953, 1955 and 1961.

Claude Decobert, chief barman since 1946, treasures his inscribed copy of Hemingway's *The Old Man and the Sea*

Above,
The front desk
in full action.

Right,
Georges Lepré,
keeper of the wines.

Opposite,
Lepré in the
dining room.

Right,
Franco Gentileschi, manager of the L'Espadon Restaurant; and (*far right*) David Campbell, reception manager since 1964.

Below,
veteran concierges Jean Mathieu (since 1953), Gérard Avez (1957), Marcel Fourmestreaux (recently retired); and (*opposite below*) Yvan Labarenne, the restaurant manager who retired in 1980 after more than forty years service.

Two views of the Ritz-Escoffier Cooking School, which is run by Gregory Usher, an American who was previously director of the Cordon Bleu and La Varenne cooking schools. The Ritz offers not only diploma courses of various kinds but also Demonstration and Master Classes.

The over-all value of the Ritz cellar has been estimated to be in excess of $1 million. A few hundred special bottles are held in numbered bins, the property of established clients who relish the fact that they maintain their own cellars at the Ritz. These bins are like numbered Swiss bank accounts: only the personnel of the *cave* know the identities of the fortunate depositors, and will not reveal their names.

One of the Ritz legends concerns the quick thinking of Hans Elmiger who saved most of these treasures from the Germans during the Second World War. Before the occupation troops arrived, most of the better vintages were moved from the hotel *cave* to the warehouse. The German residents of the Ritz, most notably Reichsmarshall

Hermann Goering, were quick to lay claim to the bottles in the hotel cellar, but knew nothing about the much more significant cache in the 15th arrondissement. Inevitably, there came the day when a German patrol insisted on seeing what was inside the warehouse. As they viewed the uncovered treasure with astonishment and undisguised anticipation, Elmiger informed them sternly that no one was permitted to partake of the Reichsmarshall's personal property. No report of the discovery was ever made to higher authorities.

The man who stands guard over the liquid treasures of the Ritz today is Georges Lepré, a *sommelier* who is gifted with an unerring ability to match wines to people. "A

HOTEL RITZ
PARIS

sommelier must be a responsible person," he says. "When people enter a room we can tell by the way they dress and act if they are very rich or somewhat less so. The very rich can afford a Margaux '61 and we can suggest it immediately. But other people must be more careful. We can sense that, and offer something more modest."

Lepré catches the keynote of the hotel he serves when he says, "You can't work at the Ritz without passion. You can't be indifferent here." One evening, Lepré watched with horror as a dinner guest in L'Espadon abruptly stood up and removed his jacket. The *sommelier* was at the table in two strides, helping the guest to put his jacket back on. "Not here, sir," he said politely but firmly.

In a sense, he was guarding not only his and his colleagues' investment, but the investment in the hotel of all those loyal, tested clients who return year after year. It is a form of fidelity that the employees of the Ritz demonstrate to a degree one does not expect from people who, after all the romance of the place is stripped away, are earning their bread and butter.

This was not always true. Until the Thirties, it was customary for concierges and others who stood to earn a great deal in tips to pay hotels for the privilege of working in them. Claude Auzello, the discipline-minded former Army officer who ran the hotel with military precision, was remembered with bitterness for the relentless tactics he used in breaking a strike of Ritz employees in the Thirties. But in the era of Charles Ritz, relationships greatly improved.

By the late Seventies, this good feeling showed signs of evaporating in the face of doubts about the hotel's future. It was clear even to those involved in the most basic services that the Ritz was on the skids. Its purchase by foreigners was perceived as a real rupture with the Ritz tradition. In addition to private concerns about continuing employment, there was apprehension about what might happen to the standards which, in the employees' own view, had set them at the pinnacle of their profession.

The cooking staff at work in the refurbished kitchen. *Inset:* Mohamed Al Fayed in toque with Guy Legay, director of cuisine.

It was Escoffier who set the Ritz's unaltered standards of attractive foods and beverages prepared by experts from the freshest possible raw materials and served with grace and attention in splendid surroundings.

But it became gratifyingly clear very soon after the change of ownership that the renovation and maintenance of the Ritz represented a calculated effort at revival – to return the hotel to those bygone standards established by César Ritz. One of his prescriptions was that the hotel maintained whatever size staff was considered essential for proper service. The cost of labour in Ritz's time obviously bore no resemblance to what it is today; to recreate those turn-of-the-century service standards is an incredibly costly proposition. In the hotel business, the normal economic ratio is two staff for every five rooms; at the Ritz today, it is 4.5 staff for every two rooms – almost exactly the reverse. Can the Ritz survive on such a seemingly uneconomic basis? Absolutely, says Frank Klein, provided he has "a fantastic product" that warrants the rates he needs to charge. The monthly turnover since 1984 would appear to bear him out; once again it is not easy to get a room at the Ritz. The ideals of César Ritz have been realized in a contemporary fashion.

Redecoration, renewal, preservation in the midst of reconstruction is one-half of the formula which maintains the world-wide pre-eminence of the Ritz; the other half is the quality of the staff. What may be unique to the Ritz is the affection that exists between clients and staff, and its intensity. Several years ago, the Gerald Beckers of Long Island, who have been coming to the Ritz for more than thirty years, were due to arrive one morning from Milan. Hours passed and they did not appear. When they finally walked into the hotel in the late afternoon – victims of an airline confusion – the receptionists and concierges, their faces grave, lined up to receive them, anxious to know if they were all right.

In 1979, after over thirty years of service, Michel Rengnez, the head concierge, was forced to retire for reasons of health. A veteran client of the Ritz, Robert Hibbert of Dallas, learned about Rengnez's illness, including plans for surgery. He did everything he could to persuade Rengnez to cancel these plans, fly with him in his private plane to Dallas and put himself under the care of a specialist there. Regnez was deeply touched by the offer but elected to have the surgery done in France. After the operation, Hibbert came to the hospital to visit the former concierge, and each year when he returned to France he called on Regnez at home.

"In no trade is the relationship between buyer and seller so close and intimate as that between client and proprietor of a hotel," César Ritz noted in the memoir he tried in vain to complete before his death. Yet even Ritz, for all the social power he came to wield and all the intimacies he shared with the august powers of his day, understood better than anyone that an inviolable space separates those who use hotels and those who operate them.

"The client is the client, the employee is the employee," according to the late reception manager Guy Moreau. Of the innumerable protocols governing the conduct of Ritz employees, the first and most symbolic is grounded in *politesse française*; always wait until the client offers his or her hand before you offer yours.

People who habitually stay at the Ritz tend to develop a proprietary attachment to it. People who work there often develop the same attachment. The feeling is somewhat like that of a club-member; in this sense, the Ritz is no less a club for veterans of the staff than it is for faithful clients.

Guy Moreau once explained that "In the normal hotel a client was a number – '135', '218'. At the Ritz, a client was nothing like that. They were Mr and Mrs or Lord and Lady So and So. We knew the names of all the members of their families. For each of them there were special things to remember – to turn off the clock if the ticking bothered them, to place a board under the mattress, the right newspaper, what breakfast they liked, so that when they arrived it was with the feeling that they had arrived in their own house. The key is the care, and because the staff don't budge, the guests are assured of the same *garçon d'étage*, the same valet, the same maid."

Moreau didn't exaggerate; the staff truly do not budge. Concierge Jean Mathieu began work at the hotel as a groom in 1953; he has never worked anywhere else. "That's not unusual," he says. "Many who come here as summer replacements spend their lives here." Bernard Azimot, the bartender known to thousands of the Ritz

Left, the Ritz Club is a membership night club which offers food and drink and music for dancing from 9 p.m. to the early hours.

Above, The Ritz is proud of its ability to provide prompt service, night and day; every client's bedside table is furnished not only with a row of buttons to summon a waiter or valet or chambermaid, but also a sophisticated telephone system adapted to the needs of the international businessman or government official. Radio and television controls are also at each bedside.

faithful as "Bertin", served four generations of one family, the William Wood-Princes of Chicago.

That sense of continuity, so rare for a transient business, pervades and shapes the Ritz client-staff relationship. Its importance to the experience for both can scarcely be overestimated. "There's only so much in the paint and the curtains. The real comfort of a hotel is in the relationship of the staff to the clients," says reception chief David Campbell, an Englishman who has been at the hotel since 1964 and is extremely popular with the guests. Among the clients, he believes there is "an incredible feeling of trust," a belief that "if anybody can help out, it's the people here who can do it."

In the old days before the advent of credit cards, assistance often included loans whenever the banks were closed, or whenever the clients' children passed through Paris on their own and found themselves short of cash. In such cases, there was never any hesitation, nor any question of an I.O.U. The same trust exists when members of the staff are handling clients' money. A client once asked Claude Decobert, the barman, to buy a car for his son, who was returning to France from the United States, and would need the car to drive to the family château in Bordeaux. For the purchase, the father sent Decobert a signed cheque, otherwise blank. After some research, Decobert finally decided on a red Simca. The dealer told him that the car could only be delivered in two weeks. Decobert placed the cheque on the table and said, "I need the car now. You tell me the figure and I will write it on the cheque." He got the car.

One client, a woman, rented a car to visit a château near Paris, then confessed to the concierges that driving frightened her. Nor would she feel comfortable being driven by a stranger. It was decided that Mathieu, whom she knew well and trusted, should drive her.

There is a Swiss gentleman who spends six months of the year at the Ritz; even when he is not in residence, he telephones David Campbell from Switzerland to make hotel arrangements for him when he travels to New York.

One of the most enduring client-employee associations on record was that between Marcel Fourmestreaux, until recently chief concierge of the Cambon side of the hotel, and Edward Mull Crump, Jr., of Memphis, Tennessee. Crump, a wealthy insurance broker, loved to sail in ocean liners to Europe. Marcel – as Fourmestreaux was known at the Ritz – was detailed by the hotel to meet Crump in Cherbourg after a 1970 crossing, and arrange to get his luggage off the liner and onto the boat train to Paris. From Cherbourg to Paris was five hours of non-stop eating and drinking in a dining car whose food was reputedly as good as Maxim's; Crump insisted that Marcel share in the feast with him, and when it was over demanded that Marcel match him, glass for glass, in drinking his favourite champagne, Veuve Cliquot.

During his stay at the hotel, Crump would summon Marcel to his room and insist that he have a whisky with him. Whenever he had a special request, it was Marcel who dealt with it. Crump was known to augment his plans for dinner as each day passed; he might initially ask for a table for twelve and end up with a party of twenty. One Sunday morning, he asked Marcel, who had earlier arranged for a dozen seats at the Hippodrome for that day, to get him another five. It was a tough assignment because the Hippodrome office was closed on Sunday, and Marcel's regular contact had the day off. Refusing to be defeated, Marcel went to the Hippodrome, found his contact's daughter, who *was* on duty that day, found the seating charts for her when she couldn't lay her hands on them, and arranged for the extra tickets.

When Marcel took Crump to his ship in 1975 for the return trip to the States, Crump refused to let him debark until the ship was about to sail, hoping to persuade him to make the voyage as his guest and fly back to Paris from New York. "If I'd been alerted before, perhaps," Marcel recalls. "But I have a wife and children."

Impromptu excursions to various parts of Europe on behalf of clients are not entirely uncommon. Marcel once flew to Geneva, then took a taxi to Lausanne to deliver a dark suit, shirt and tie to a Saudi Arabian, a client of the Ritz, who needed them for a dinner he was to attend that evening. The wife of a French nobleman sent Mathieu to London to retrieve a key she'd forgotten, to Madrid to deliver some film to a friend and to Monte Carlo to pick up a valise she'd left on a boat. Gérard Avez, the present chief concierge, travelled to London to fetch $400,000 in jewels back to the Ritz for safekeeping; the jewels were owned by an American client who was about to depart for Russia and was afraid to take them with her.

Most clients in most hotels – even those in the top echelon – take the staff for granted, noticing them for the most part only when something goes wrong. At the Ritz that is not and never has been the case – and therein may lie the ingredient that makes the Ritz so special in the eyes of its clientèle.

When a veteran client returns to the Ritz and is greeted by members of the hotel staff he or she has known for years, it is a human, not a commercial transaction that is

taking place. Bertin, the beloved barman who used to squire groups of Ritz clients to major rugby matches, maintains that the intimacy between clients and staff is what gives the Ritz "cachet". Perhaps "sense of family" is more descriptive of what exists. Whatever it is, this uncommon bond has been there since the time of César Ritz, and is for many clients the greatest attraction of the hotel.

Marie-Louise Ritz is supposed to have said, "This is our immortality." As it nears a century of existence, the Ritz Hotel continues to stand in the Place Vendôme, in the centre of almost everyone's favourite city, a repository of social history without parallel in the world. Threatened with a kind of eclipse, it has been infused by Mr Al Fayed with new life – and in a manner that honours the past as much as it salutes the present.

The miracle of the Ritz is that this palace created for princes feels so truly and immediately like home to commoners. But what a home it is, and what a history it holds! A stay at the Ritz may be old hat for princes, as well as for kings of commerce and art, but for the commoners among us it provides a taste of life as we had always imagined it could be.

Opposite:
The gracious curving staircase that leads down from the lobby to the Health Club.

A selection of signatures from the Ritz's special guest book, the *Livre d'or:*

Maria Callas

Greta Garbo

Paul Getty

Barbara Hutton

Janet Flanner

Baroness Kuffner (Tamara de Lempicka)

Jack Hemingway

Margaux Hemingway

Mariel Hemingway

Sir Charles and Lady Chaplin

Igor Stravinsky

M. Gulbenkian

The Duke and Duchess of Windsor

Nana Mouskouri

Earl and Countess Spencer

Leontyne Price

Rudolph Nureyev

Natalia Makarova

Oscar de la Renta

Bill Blass

Wm. Randolph Hearst

Orson Welles

Richard Burton and Elizabeth Taylor

Valentino

Harold Robbins

Gloria Vanderbilt

Danny Kaye

Glenn Ford

Woody Allen

Claudia Cardinale

Gene Kelly

Ursula Andress

Elsa Martinelli

Dr. Henry A. Kissinger

Michael York

Their Majesties the King and Queen of Norway

His Majesty King Hassan II of Morocco

David Rockefeller

Gregory Peck

The Prince and Princess of Thurn und Taxis

Celebrated people relax at the Ritz; *right,* Henry Kissinger; *opposite,* Catherine Deneuve.

Elton John

Barbra Streisand

Lana Turner

Barbara Cartland

Prince and Princess Rainier of Monaco

Robert Wagner

President Richard Nixon

Andy Williams

Mick Jagger

Patrick Duffy

Cheryl Tiegs and Peter Beard

David Essex

Placido Domingo

Rex Harrison

Jessye Norman

Donna Summer

Franz Beckenbauer

Pelé

Her Majesty Queen Nour al Hussein of Jordan

Pierre Elliot Trudeau

President and Mrs. Gerald Ford

Peter Hoffmann

Judith Krantz

James Coburn

Lauren Bacall

Warren Beatty

Jack Lemmon

Walter Matthau

Kirk Douglas

Marc Chagall

Dean Martin

Dustin Hoffman

Michael Cimino

Louis Jourdan

Rock Hudson

Esther Williams

The popular British novelist Barbara Cartland, a perennial guest since the 1920s, receives a courtly greeting at the entrance to the Ritz from the photographer Norman Parkinson. *Opposite*, the Begum Aly Khan at home in her sitting-room at the Ritz.

Victoria Principal

Olivia Newton John

Her Majesty Queen Ileana of Rumania

Sir Georg Solti

Paul Anka

Sir David Lean

Their Majesties the King and Queen of Greece

Yasmin Aga Khan (Mme Embiricos)

Marisa Berenson

Joan Collins

John D. Rockefeller IV

Rod Stewart

Debbie Reynolds

Roger Moore

Itzhak Perlman

Monseigneur le Comte Henri de Paris

His Majesty The Sultan of Brunei Darussalam

Their Highnesses Prince Karim and Bégum Aga Khan

Prince and Princess Sadruddin Aga Khan

John and Lady Aspinall

Princess Ann Mari von Bismarck

Count and Countess Maximilian von Bismarck

Joan Baez

Mrs. Vincent Astor

Mr. and Mrs. Giovanni Agnelli

Grace, Lady Dudley

Sir John and Lady Dunlop

Princess Teresa von Fuerstenberg

Prince and Princess Joachim von Fuerstenberg

Princess Diane von Fuerstenberg

Princess Ira von Fuerstenberg

Ambassador and Mrs. Charles Price

Charles Collingwood

Eddie Constantine

Prof. John K. Galbraith

Baron Guy de Gunzburg

Baron Alain de Gunzburg

Mr. and Mrs. Gordon Getty

Serge Gainsbourg

Ambassador and Mrs. Walter Annenberg

Lee Iacocca

Quincy Jones

Efrem Kurtz

Lord and Lady Lever

Prince and Princess Rupert Lowenstein

Prince and Princess Edouard Lobkowicz

Marquis Raimondo de Larrain

Rolf Liebermann

INDEX

Page numbers in italics refer to illustration captions.

I am Ritzy